Shining Lights

Workbook 7
C1+

Jo Cummins   Helen Chilton

Shaftesbury Road, Cambridge CB2 8EA, United Kingdom

One Liberty Plaza, 20th Floor, New York, NY 10006, USA

477 Williamstown Road, Port Melbourne, VIC 3207, Australia

314–321, 3rd Floor, Plot 3, Splendor Forum, Jasola District Centre, New Delhi – 110025, India

103 Penang Road, #05–06/07, Visioncrest Commercial, Singapore 238467

Cambridge University Press & Assessment is a department of the University of Cambridge.

We share the University's mission to contribute to society through the pursuit of education, learning and research at the highest international levels of excellence.

www.cambridge.org
Information on this title: www.cambridge.org/9781009232418

© Cambridge University Press & Assessment 2026

This publication is in copyright. Subject to statutory exception and to the provisions of relevant collective licensing agreements, no reproduction of any part may take place without the written permission of Cambridge University Press & Assessment.

First published 2026
20 19 18 17 16 15 14 13 12 11 10 9 8 7 6 5 4 3 2 1

Printed in Poland by Opolgraf

A catalogue record for this publication is available from the British Library

ISBN   978-1-009-23241-8   Workbook with Digital Pack

Additional resources for this publication at www.cambridge.org/shininglights

Cambridge University Press & Assessment has no responsibility for the persistence or accuracy of URLs for external or third-party internet websites referred to in this publication and does not guarantee that any content on such websites is, or will remain, accurate or appropriate.

CONTENTS

UNIT 1: Working it out — page 4

UNIT 2: Body positive — page 12

UNIT 3: Food for thought — page 20

REVIEW 1: Units 1, 2 & 3 — page 28

UNIT 4: Among friends — page 32

UNIT 5: Time out — page 40

UNIT 6: What's in a word? — page 48

REVIEW 2: Units 4, 5 & 6 — page 56

UNIT 7: Community spirit — page 60

UNIT 8: It's not fair! — page 68

UNIT 9: The fame game — page 76

REVIEW 3: Units 7, 8 & 9 — page 84

EXPLORING EMPLOYABILITY — page 88

VOCABULARY BUILDER — page 96

TOWARDS PROFICIENCY — page 105

IRREGULAR VERBS — page 111

UNIT 1 WORKING IT OUT

VOCABULARY

EXPRESSING CHANGE

1 Complete the phrases with the words in the box.

> beyond change circumstances dramatic
> fresh same scratch shift sweeping
> times transformation unchanged

1. experience a gradual _____
2. bring about a _____ change
3. move with the _____
4. undergo a complete _____
5. stay the _____
6. make _____ changes
7. adapt to changing _____
8. remain _____
9. make a _____ start
10. start again from _____
11. change _____ recognition
12. see a slow but steady _____

2 Complete the job advert with the phrases in Exercise 1. You may need to change the form of the verb. Some phrases can go in more than one place, but use each option only once.

> Are you looking to ¹ _____ ?
> Are you someone who easily
> ² _____ ?
>
> We're looking for a new sales and marketing executive to help us ³ _____
> to the way we advertise our technology business. We're a company that tries to
> ⁴ _____ , so we need someone who is up-to-date with the latest social media trends. Now is a great time to join our company as it ⁵ _____ .

READING

1 You are going to read an article about people whose career ambitions changed. What reasons can you think of for this happening?

2 Scan the texts and find the reason why each person did not end up pursuing their childhood career ambitions.

EXAM TIP

Underline the key words in each of the questions. Then read through the texts carefully, looking for similar ideas to those in the questions. Underline words or sentences that help give the answers.

3 Look at question 5 in the exam task and underline the key words. Then read text A and underline the words or sentences that answer the question.

EXAM TASK — READING AND USE OF ENGLISH PART 8

4 You are going to read an article in which four professionals discuss how their career ambitions have changed. For questions 1–10, choose from the professionals (A–D). The professionals may be chosen more than once.

Which professional

has not completely abandoned a former habit?	1
lacked knowledge of the approach they should take to fulfil their ambition?	2
was forced to switch career due to circumstances beyond their control?	3
was unconcerned about their failure to make headway in a chosen field?	4
changed their mind as a result of seeing the reality of a particular job?	5
had a particularly strong ambition to achieve great success?	6
transferred their acquired knowledge of a subject to a related career?	7
refocussed their ambitions after discovering a hidden talent?	8
eventually realised that they were not as talented as they had believed?	9
imagined that the career they thought about following was always improbable?	10

Changing career ambitions

Four professionals talk about how their career ambitions changed

A Magda Nowak

Until I was eight, my family lived directly under the flight path of a nearby airport and I'd often stand watching planes being launched into the sky above my head. Back then, there was never any question of me becoming anything other than a pilot and that remained unchanged for many years. It wasn't until I took my first flight as a passenger when I was a young adult that my dreams of living a life in the skies were torn apart. The inside of the cabin was barely as comfortable as an inter-city bus, and the pilot was simply a driver, transporting people from A to B. To say I was disappointed is an understatement. I'd poured my heart and soul into studying the physics of flying and the mechanics of planes. There was nothing for it but to apply all that to the next best thing, and I embarked on what has since become a highly satisfying career as an aircraft engineer.

B David Torres

Like many young people, I would often drift off into the realms of fantasy about life as a social media influencer, wafting around in clothes handed to me freely by those eager to get a mention in my feeds. Deep down, I knew it was unrealistic and I'd likely end up doing something more mundane. And I certainly never considered the need to act on things, for example, build a following. My daily updates were going no further than my friends' eyes, and the truth of the matter was that I hadn't the first idea how to boost my online presence – the practicalities of influencing were beyond me. The idea faded as I took a liking to technical drawing at college, and unexpectedly found myself excelling at it. This brought about a dramatic change in my life. I concentrated my efforts on my studies and potential future career. I'm currently studying to be an architect and finally have a clear direction.

C Olly Brown

I saw a documentary about psychologists once as a teenager and instantly knew it was the role for me, convinced I was highly intuitive and could read people like books. I'd even practise my 'personality readings' on friends. It was much later before it clicked that they had simply been indulging me, that I possessed no extraordinary aptitude for understanding the way in which people's minds worked. That was compounded by achieving only mediocre results in psychology assignments at college, despite my keen efforts. Fortunately, I'm very laid-back, so I just shrugged it off and made a fresh start. If I wasn't going to be scrutinising people's thoughts and feelings for a living, I'd turn my attention to another interest: computer programming. I completed the relevant course of study and am now happily ensconced in the role of product developer for a tech company, though I have to admit to carrying out amateur analyses of colleagues' personality traits. I just keep my observations to myself now!

D Beatrice Abadie

Dance: that's all I ever wanted to do, and I was aiming extremely high – nothing less than prima ballerina for a prestigious ballet company was going to satisfy me. And I was good. Then one day, I slipped on an overly-polished studio floor after another dancer accidentally bumped into me and took a tumble. The resulting injury laid me up for weeks. On my eventual return to the studio, I understood that I would always have a weakness in one ankle. My dancing days were over. I won't deny that I took it hard, and it was several months before I acknowledged I'd have to put my dreams behind me and accept that the life I'd imagined spreading out before me had changed beyond recognition. What could I do instead? Becoming a ballet instructor was out of the question. If I couldn't dance, I couldn't bear to watch someone else take my place on the stage. Instead, I retrained as a beauty therapist and now run a small yet busy salon in my home town.

GRAMMAR
FUTURE TENSES

1 Match the sentences 1–8 to the tenses a–h.

1. If this company keeps losing money, it isn't going to exist next year.
2. I'll be working from home all next week.
3. Your shift doesn't finish until 7 pm.
4. Many experts think that there'll be no more factory workers in 50 years' time.
5. Will you have finished the report by tomorrow?
6. Next year, the company will have been trading for over one hundred years.
7. The company is currently undergoing a transformation in its management structure.
8. I'll send you the files this afternoon.

a future perfect
b future simple
c future continuous
d *going to*
e present continuous
f present simple
g *will* + infinitive
h future perfect continuous

2 Choose the correct options to complete the text.

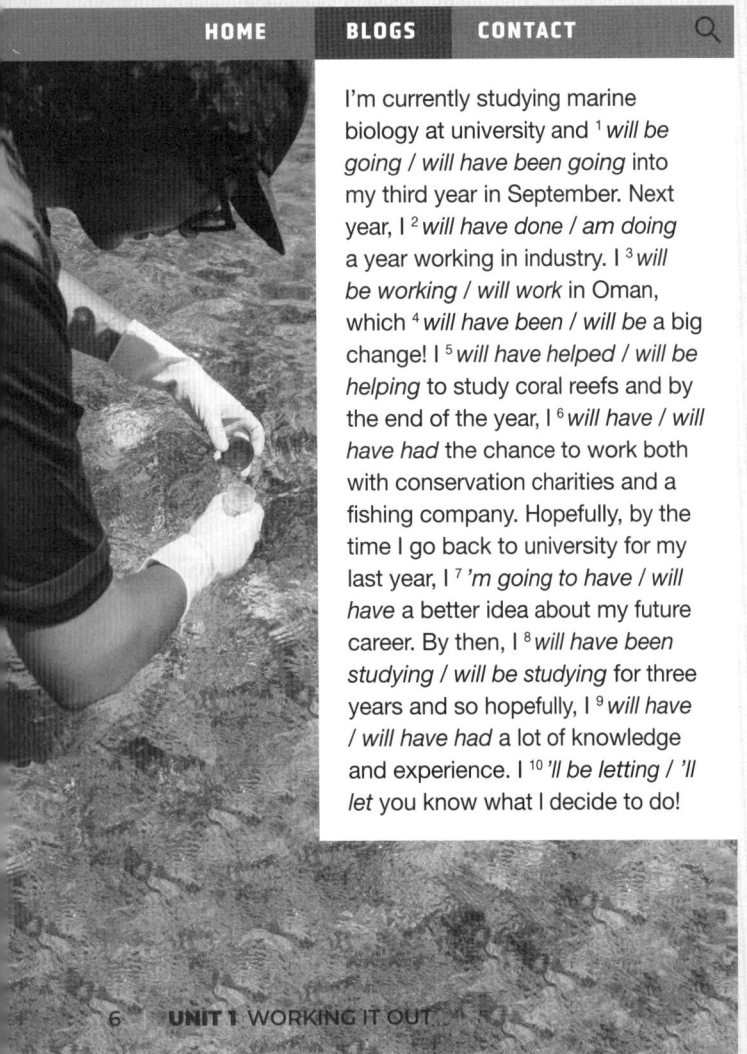

HOME | BLOGS | CONTACT

I'm currently studying marine biology at university and ¹ *will be going / will have been going* into my third year in September. Next year, I ² *will have done / am doing* a year working in industry. I ³ *will be working / will work* in Oman, which ⁴ *will have been / will be* a big change! I ⁵ *will have helped / will be helping* to study coral reefs and by the end of the year, I ⁶ *will have / will have had* the chance to work both with conservation charities and a fishing company. Hopefully, by the time I go back to university for my last year, I ⁷ *'m going to have / will have* a better idea about my future career. By then, I ⁸ *will have been studying / will be studying* for three years and so hopefully, I ⁹ *will have / will have had* a lot of knowledge and experience. I ¹⁰ *'ll be letting / 'll let* you know what I decide to do!

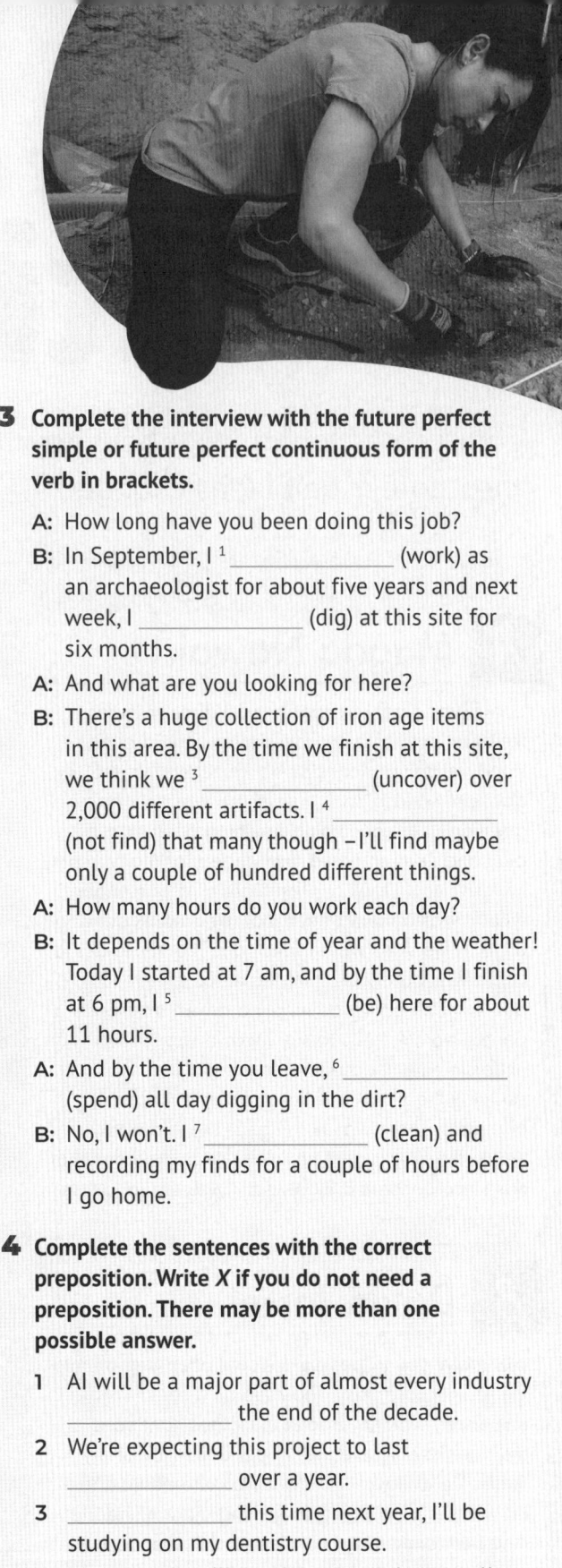

3 Complete the interview with the future perfect simple or future perfect continuous form of the verb in brackets.

A: How long have you been doing this job?
B: In September, I ¹ _____ (work) as an archaeologist for about five years and next week, I _____ (dig) at this site for six months.
A: And what are you looking for here?
B: There's a huge collection of iron age items in this area. By the time we finish at this site, we think we ³ _____ (uncover) over 2,000 different artifacts. I ⁴ _____ (not find) that many though – I'll find maybe only a couple of hundred different things.
A: How many hours do you work each day?
B: It depends on the time of year and the weather! Today I started at 7 am, and by the time I finish at 6 pm, I ⁵ _____ (be) here for about 11 hours.
A: And by the time you leave, ⁶ _____ (spend) all day digging in the dirt?
B: No, I won't. I ⁷ _____ (clean) and recording my finds for a couple of hours before I go home.

4 Complete the sentences with the correct preposition. Write *X* if you do not need a preposition. There may be more than one possible answer.

1. AI will be a major part of almost every industry _____ the end of the decade.
2. We're expecting this project to last _____ over a year.
3. _____ this time next year, I'll be studying on my dentistry course.
4. My new role will require me to take an online course _____ the same time as working full time.
5. _____ the coming few years, the company needs to make sweeping changes.
6. How much time will you spend _____ updating your CV this year?
7. I'm hoping to get a promotion _____ the next year or so.

OTHER WAYS TO TALK ABOUT THE FUTURE

5 Match the sentence halves.

1 The company is on the verge of
2 As part of this expansion, the management are about to
3 If you are looking for a new role, the company is
4 There are also bound to be
5 They are set to

a expanding into the European market.
b many opportunities for existing staff that want to further their career.
c announce the opening of a new office in Milan.
d make the biggest profits they have ever made.
e to advertise for staff to work in these offices.

6 Complete the blog with the phrases in Exercise 5. Sometimes there is more than one possible answer.

I'm ¹_____ start the next stage of my training to become a firefighter. I'm ²_____ submitting my online tests, and tomorrow I'm attending the fitness assessment. It ³_____ quite hard as it's a physical job, but I've been training hard. The first task ⁴_____ be a running test, and then we have to climb ladders and show we can lift equipment. Last month, I was ⁵_____ giving up because I hurt my back. It's much better now though, so I think I ⁶_____ go!

7 Complete the sentences with your own ideas.

1 I'm on the verge of _____.
2 We are about to _____.
3 My teacher is bound to _____.
4 I am set to _____.
5 The world is on the point of _____.

8 >>> **STRETCH!** Complete the second sentence so that it has the same meaning to the first, using the word given.

1 I'm sure he's going to get the job.
   He's _____. **BOUND**
2 I'm finishing my degree in September.
   By November, _____. **WILL**
3 She's about to quit her job.
   She's _____. **VERGE**
4 I'm working for my mum's business next week.
   This time next week, _____. **BE**
5 We're going to open a careers service next year.
   We're _____. **SET**

VOCABULARY
PHRASAL VERBS

1 Choose the correct answers.

1 Have you seen Abdul's new car? He must really be *raking in / falling into* the money.
2 Despite *heading off / plugging away* at her YouTube channel for years, Amina still only has a couple of hundred subscribers.
3 I'm really interested to see what the next new development to *wipe out / shake up* the tech industry will be.
4 I'm not sure how I became an influencer – I just *fell into / did away with* it, really.
5 If I don't find a new job soon, I might have to *lay off / resort to* asking my brother for a loan.
6 Our new software system will mean that we can *do away with / rake in* a lot of paperwork.
7 Sorry – I'm going to have to *head off / shake up* because I have a meeting.
8 I'm really worried I might be *resorted to / laid off* soon as our company isn't doing very well.
9 My computer just crashed and *wiped out / plugged away* all the work I did today.

2 Answer the questions with your own ideas.

1 What do you think is the best way to rake in lots of money quickly?
2 What is something you would like to do away with? Why?
3 Have you ever accidentally wiped out all your work?
4 What is something you have been plugging away at for a while?
5 Which industry do you think needs a shake up? Why?

LISTENING

1. Read the title of the text in the exam task. What does a bicycle courier do?

EXAM TIP

Remember that you may need to write more than one word for your answers, and should not change the form of the words you hear.

2. Read sentences 1–8 in the exam task. What word, or kind of word, might go in each gap?

EXAM TASK — LISTENING PART 2

3. 🔊 1.1 You will hear a woman called Joanna Thompson talking about her work as a bicycle courier. For questions 1–8, complete the sentences with a word or short phrase.

WORKING AS A BICYCLE COURIER

Joanna says the most important advantage of bicycle couriers for companies are the (1) _____ benefits.

The most unusual thing Joanna has delivered was some (2) _____.

During journeys around the city, (3) _____ get in Joanna's way most often.

Joanna never fails to check that she has her (4) _____ before leaving home each day.

The worst weather Joanna has encountered while working was an unexpected (5) _____.

Joanna became stuck in a (6) _____ on one occasion, which she found amusing.

Joanna is currently deciding whether to take up the opportunity of delivering (7) _____.

Joanna has been surprised by how her (8) _____ have been impacted by cycling.

WRITING

A PROPOSAL

1. Why might researching potential careers be useful to people finishing their education? What kind of information might a young person look up?

2. Read the writing task below and answer the questions.
   1. Who is the target audience of the proposal?
   2. What tone should you use: formal, neutral or informal?
   3. How many points do you need to address in your answer? What are they?

> You would like students to spend a day researching potential career options and their entry requirements. You decide to write a proposal to your headteacher in which you describe how the day might be organised, explain what kinds of jobs students might explore, and justify why it is worth taking time out from ordinary lessons to do the research.

3 Read the proposal. Which of the following functions does the writer use?

- describing
- suggesting
- explaining
- enquiring
- persuading
- recommending

1 _____

As many of the older students are about to start considering their career options, it would be of huge benefit to them to learn about the kinds of jobs that are out there and how they might take appropriate steps to securing a position in their chosen field.

2 _____

The computer room is often free all day on Mondays, and this would be the perfect opportunity for students to use the available resources. There could be teacher-guided sessions, where students are given helpful tasks, such as completing questionnaires about their strengths and weaknesses, or personality quizzes.

3 _____

Students may not have a good knowledge of the kinds of jobs that ordinary people do, and many are already focussing their ambitions on exciting-sounding roles such as social media influencer or footballer. With help focussing on their individual skills and qualities, they might discover less popular and competitive jobs that are equally interesting, which would bring about a dramatic change in their thinking.

4 _____

Having time to explore career options with professional help from a teacher or other experienced adult will certainly be of value to students who do not have a clear direction to work towards. Missing a day of ordinary classes will be a small price to pay for being better prepared for life beyond school.

5 _____

To sum up, offering students the chance to consider their future working life during a work research day would give them a clearer picture of how to go about finding the role that is right for them.

4 Write headings for paragraphs 1–5 in the proposal.

EXAM TIP

Read the task carefully. Underline the points to address in your answer and make brief notes on them. Make sure you write a similar amount for each of the points in your answer.

5 Read the exam task. Make notes about each of the three points you should address in your answer.

✓ EXAM TASK WRITING PART 2

You think it would be useful for students at your college to gain work experience in a local business for a week.

You decide to write a proposal to your college principal in which you explain what fields of work students might be most interested in, how doing work experience would benefit students, and what advantages there might be for companies who choose to take part.

Write your **proposal**.

6 Write your answer in 220–260 words in an appropriate style.

7 💼 **Professional Development and Management**
Have you ever done any work experience?
If yes, what did you do? What skills did you learn? How do you think it will help you in the future?
If no, what would you like to do if you could do work experience? Why?

SELF-EVALUATION

Check your writing:

Content: Have you addressed all three points fully, providing reasons for your ideas? ☹ ☺ 😐 😊

Communication: Have you communicated your ideas in an effective way? ☹ ☺ 😐 😊

Organisation: Is your proposal well-organised, with a variety of cohesive devices? ☹ ☺ 😐 😊

Language: Have you used a range of vocabulary and grammatical structures accurately? ☹ ☺ 😐 😊

INTERVIEW SKILLS

Have you ever had an interview (e.g. for a job, school course, volunteering role, etc)? What was it like?
How do you feel about having interviews in the future?

1 CONTROLLING MY VOICE

Things I need to think about (e.g. volume, speed, etc):
_____
_____

Ideas from the class discussion and the video:
_____
_____

2 USING APPROPRIATE LANGUAGE AND REGISTER

New phrases I want to use: _____
_____

A phrase I could use to ask for clarification: _____

A phrase I could use to buy time: _____
_____

Phrases I shouldn't use: _____
_____

3 MAINTAINING FOCUS, PLANNING AND ADAPTING TO THE SITUATION

How do you deal with stressful situations? Can you think of one you've experienced? What happened? What could you do to stay calm before an interview?

Things that could go wrong	How I could deal with them

10 | UNIT 1 WORKING IT OUT

ORACY 1

My role play partner is: _____

I work for: _____

Questions for my partner:

_____

_____

_____

_____

I'm being interviewed for a job at: _____

Notes for my interview:

_____

_____

_____

_____

Why not record your interviews so you can watch them again? You might notice things that you need to work on, as well as things you did well.

Reflections on the interview

Things that went well:

_____

_____

Things that could be improved:

_____

_____

How I used my voice and language effectively:

_____

_____

Things we did well as a group:

_____

_____

How I maintained focus and dealt with anything unexpected:

_____

_____

Try swapping and interviewing for the other job. Think about improving the things you noted above.

SELF-EVALUATION

I can ...
- control the volume of my voice.
- use appropriate language and register according to the context.
- maintain focus and plan the points I want to make.
- use appropriate body language and eye contact.
- adapt my approach to the situation.

UNIT 1 WORKING IT OUT | 11

UNIT 2 BODY POSITIVE

VOCABULARY

BODY IDIOMS

1 Complete the body idioms.

1. go _____ your head
2. make your _____ boil
3. have a _____ of heart
4. _____ someone's arm
5. get _____ feet
6. breathe down someone's _____
7. bite your _____
8. pick someone's _____
9. get something off your _____
10. _____ your mind

2 Complete the second sentence so that it has a similar meaning to the first, using the correct form of a phrase in Exercise 1.

1. I heard something yesterday that amazed me!
   I heard something yesterday that _____.
2. Can I persuade you to come to the gym?
   Can I _____ to come to the gym?
3. I didn't understand that film at all.
   That film _____.
4. Can I ask your opinion on something?
   Can I _____ about something?
5. I need to talk to you about something that has been annoying me for a while.
   I need to _____.

READING

1 Read the title of the article. Who might the target audience be?

EXAM TIP

The questions are in the same order as the information in the text.

EXAM TASK — READING AND USE OF ENGLISH PART 5

2 You are going to read an article about exercise. For questions 1–6, choose the answer (A, B, C or D) which you think fits best according to the text.

1. What is the writer doing in the first paragraph?
   A expressing doubt about the reason for the high cost of gym memberships
   B showing sympathy for those who dislike the idea of going to the gym
   C acknowledging that going to the gym is as good a form of exercise as any other
   D discussing the characteristics of those who prefer the gym over other types of exercise

2. What does the writer say about swimming?
   A It is gentle exercise that slowly builds strength.
   B It requires participants to have robust self-esteem.
   C It ought to be recommended to less mobile people.
   D It is generally less popular in cooler climates.

3. What are compared in the second paragraph?
   A choices of location available to swimmers
   B benefits of swimming for various health issues
   C differing attitudes towards swimming
   D unusual conditions swimmers might experience

4. What is the writer's main purpose in the third paragraph?
   A to highlight studies carried out into the benefits of walking
   B to explain that there is little reason to avoid walking as an activity
   C to justify walking in unpleasant conditions
   D to emphasise the challenges of walking

5. What does the writer say can be difficult about housework as exercise?
   A identifying jobs that require more energy
   B staying engaged during more mundane jobs
   C achieving recommended movement levels
   D finding the motivation to do it regularly

6. What point does the writer make about the activities referred to in the final paragraph?
   A They enable housebound people to stay active.
   B They encourage employees to engage more fully with their work.
   C They represent an approach that healthcare workers can adopt.
   D They hide the fact movement is taking place.

THE BEST FORMS OF <u>EXERCISE</u> FOR THE LEAST AMOUNT OF *effort*

Walking into a gym can be intimidating: all those super-toned gym bunnies sweating it out on the treadmills and rowing machines is enough to make anyone have a change of heart, let alone those of us who've never set foot in a gym before. The good news is that some of the most beneficial forms of exercise require neither nerves of steel nor a very positive bank balance to splash out on substantial fees. All they demand is a little enthusiasm, some comfortable gear, and the determination to invest a bit of time and enough energy into getting fitter.

Often considered the best form of exercise is swimming. Working against the resistance of the water over time gradually promotes power and fitness, and its buoyancy provides support for those for whom weight-bearing exercise would cause more harm than good – people with joint problems like arthritis, for example. This low-impact exercise is a winner for those willing to put on a bathing suit and float in water, wherever that may be. However, for those less inclined to squeeze themselves into form-fitting Lycra in an overheated swimming pool changing room before getting into what invariably feels like the ocean in the middle of winter, or for those whose skin or lungs react badly to chemicals, there are of course lakes and the sea. But for anyone reluctant to get into any kind of water, there are other, kinder options.

Walking is something the majority of us can do, providing we have appropriate footwear and somewhere to go. Truth be told, it's difficult to rule oneself out of both categories. Walking's free, helps us maintain a healthy weight and offers huge cardiovascular benefits. Evidence-based research shows that it has a positive impact on mental health and reduces the risk of experiencing age-related memory loss. In fact, the benefits of walking compared to the effects of being a couch potato will blow your mind. What's more, if breathtaking views and pollutant-free air aren't really on the agenda in your corner of the world, you'll at the very least have the opportunity to observe your local environment more closely, whatever form it takes. And while some might complain about rain and muddy ground, bear in the mind the old expression, 'There's no such thing as bad weather, only bad clothing'.

There will always be those of us who just cannot be convinced to do anything resembling structured exercise, but this doesn't mean we're a lost cause when it comes to staying fit. Most of us have to keep on top of household chores: vacuuming, tidying, making beds, cleaning vehicles and windows, mowing lawns, loading the dishwasher. Even pushing a trolley round the supermarket before loading the shopping into the boot of the car has its merits. The only potential downside is fitting enough domestic tasks in to satisfy the doctors who advise at least 150 minutes of moderate exercise a week. However, given the number of tasks the average household requires to remain tidy and dirt-free – and who really wants to be surrounded by piles of dishes or unswept floors – this is unquestionably doable. Wandering about dusting bits of furniture won't cut it: there needs to be at least a little hard work involved, a little effort to raise the heartbeat.

Even those who both avoid traditional exercise and really don't care about a messy house can be persuaded into moving if it is presented as entertainment. Playing catch with younger siblings, joining in active video games that get you off the sofa, and waving your arms to your favourite beats can all be counted as exercise without the appearance of being so. And since such activity generally takes place within your own four walls, this means minimal disruption to your daily routine. Exercise can even pass under the radar at work: the walks between car and office, regular trips to the water dispenser or canteen. And if you have a forward-thinking boss, stand-up desks and walking meetings, whose primary aim is not to incorporate movement into the working day but to stimulate creativity or ease the physical discomfort of being bent over a computer all day, can also play their part – and keep your doctor happy.

GRAMMAR

NO, NOT, NONE, NEITHER AND NOR

1 Complete the sentences with *no*, *not*, *none*, *neither* or *nor*.

1 Chama got _____ sleep whatsoever last night.
2 _____ me _____ my sister like eating vegetables.
3 He thinks going to the gym is _____ better than running.
4 Akira tried two different exercise classes last week, but _____ of them were for him.
5 I wanted to buy some fruit, but the shop had _____ left.
6 My brothers don't like any exercise. _____ swimming, _____ football – nothing!

2 Find and correct five errors in the text.

Most of my friends would tell you I'm none different to them. I like computer games, tennis and listening to music. I love watching football, but no playing it. That's OK because no of my two best friends like playing it, neither Nadia or Dario. We all enjoy different activities, but none in the same way. Some of us love hiking in the mountains, while others prefer reading a good book. No of us should feel pressured to follow the same hobbies. Embracing our differences makes life richer and more beautiful.

3 Write three sentences of your own with *no*, *not*, *none*, *neither* or *nor*.

CONDITIONAL CONCEPTS

4 Match the sentence halves.

1 Unless you have completed the training session,
2 Providing that you have filled in all the forms,
3 Imagine being able to
4 If you were to have an injury in the gym,
5 You should always sign up for classes online,
6 As long as you have no health problems,
7 Suppose you want to try a new class,

a swim every day, all year round.
b you can't use the gym equipment.
c otherwise there might not be space for you.
d you can just check the timetable on the app.
e a member of staff will always be here to help you.
f anyone can use the sauna.
g you can start using the facilities immediately.

5 Complete the text with the words and phrases in the box. Sometimes there is more than one possible answer.

> as long as   if you were   imagine   otherwise
> providing   provided that   supposing   supposing that

The LAZY person's guide to exercise

¹_____ being fit, healthy and always full of energy … sounds great, right? But, there's just one problem – you hate sport and going to the gym! Don't worry, ²_____ you're willing to make a few small changes to your lifestyle, you can get more active.

For a start, ³_____ to walk or cycle to school or work, then you could both save money and get fit. This only works ⁴_____ you live close enough to do this, though. ⁵_____, why not get off the bus a few stops early and walk the rest of the journey? Another easy change is to choose the stairs and not the lift. ⁶_____ you climb a few flights of stairs a day, you could get more exercise than going for a run.

Another great way to exercise is dancing, so grab some friends and go for a night out! ⁷_____ you're having fun, you won't even notice you're getting fit!

6 Complete the sentences with your own ideas.

1 If I were to do one thing to improve my health, _____.
2 I wouldn't eat _____ unless _____.
3 I normally sleep for _____ a night provided that _____.
4 Most people can get fit as long as _____.
5 Supposing I am healthy, _____.
6 I _____ every day, otherwise _____.

7 >>> STRETCH! Complete the email with one word in each gap.

> < Inbox   2 Messages   ∧ ∨
>
> Hi Uncle Max,
>
> Sorry I didn't help you with your house move today. To be honest, I haven't been feeling very good lately because I'm ¹_____ sleeping well. Last night I had ²_____ sleep whatsoever! Mum says that ³_____ I start sleeping better, I should go to the doctor. I've tried exercising, meditation apps, going to bed earlier, going to bed later – ⁴_____ of them help!
>
> Anyway, hopefully I'll see you at football tomorrow, but ⁵_____ I hope to come to your party next week – as ⁶_____ as I've had some sleep by then!
>
> Love, Sergio

VOCABULARY
HEALTH COLLOCATIONS

1 Emotional Intelligence Complete the questions with the correct form of the verbs in the box.

> avoid be boost build get have
> maintain reduce require respond suffer

1 What is something you do to _____ your stress levels?
2 Have you ever _____ emergency medical attention?
3 Do you know anyone who _____ from a chronic disease?
4 What do you think is the best way to _____ plenty of exercise?
5 Do you think you _____ in good or poor health?
6 Are there any processed foods you try to _____?
7 What do you think is the best way to _____ someone's mental health?
8 Have you ever _____ an adverse side effect to anything?
9 Do you think you are good at _____ a positive attitude?
10 If a member of your family had been sick, how would you help them to _____ up their strength again?
11 Do you normally _____ well to common treatments such as painkillers?

2 Write your answers to the questions in Exercise 1.

3 Critical Thinking and Decision Making
In some cultures, you are expected to go to work or school even when you are unwell to show your commitment. However, in other cultures sick people usually stay at home so they don't spread their illnesses. What do people do in your culture? Which approach do you think is better, and why?

LISTENING

1 Read the definitions. Which describes an opinion? Which describes an attitude?

1 how you think or feel about something and how this makes you behave _____
2 a thought or belief about someone or something _____

2 Which of the examples below show a speaker's attitude? Which show an opinion?

1 'I regret not taking better care of my health when I was younger.'
2 'The idea that diseases can be cured through healthy eating is nonsense.'
3 'Joining a sports centre is a complete waste of time. I can just as easily exercise at home.'
4 'I'm grateful that I sleep so well compared to other people of my age.'

EXAM TIP

Listen carefully to what each speaker says in the three dialogues. During the first listening, choose the answer you think is correct. Use the second listening to confirm your answer.

3 Match the terms in the dialogues 1–3 to the definitions a–c.

1 dietary supplements
2 nutritional psychiatry
3 superfoods

a a field of mental health that focuses on how what we eat affects us
b products like vitamins and minerals that aim to promote physical and mental well-being
c items to eat that are considered particularly nutritious

4 Read the context sentence for Extracts One to Three in the exam task, then underline the key words in the questions and options.

EXAM TASK LISTENING PART 1

5 🔊 2.1 You will hear three different extracts. For questions 1–6, choose the answer (A, B or C) which fits best according to what you hear. There are two questions for each extract.

Extract One

You hear a man and a woman talking about supplementary vitamins and minerals.

1 What is the woman's opinion about taking dietary supplements?
   A Not every vitamin and mineral can be found in everyday meals.
   B People might as well give them the benefit of the doubt.
   C They are only of value in exceptional circumstances.

2 The woman says that our ability to absorb supplements
   A is the exception rather than the rule.
   B is dependent on several factors.
   C is the subject of much discussion.

Extract Two

You hear two nutritionists discussing a new field of mental health called nutritional psychiatry.

3 What is the woman's attitude towards nutritional psychiatry?
   A hopeful that it may have wide-ranging impact
   B regretful about its potential impact on one profession
   C concerned about the reality of implementing its recommendations

4 When talking about the gut as a 'second brain', the man reveals his
   A scepticism of the results of studies into the impact of diet on mental health.
   B frustration regarding exaggerated claims made about diet.
   C reluctance to recommend relying on diet to certain people.

Extract Three

You hear two friends talking about 'superfoods', which people believe have excellent health benefits.

5 The speakers agree that
   A the same foods can fall into both healthy and unhealthy categories.
   B what matters is how much of certain foods we consume.
   C there is no such thing as a completely bad food.

6 What does the woman do during the conversation?
   A suggest alternatives to foods the man dislikes
   B dismiss the man's general approach to eating
   C correct the man's beliefs about specific foods

WRITING

A REPORT

1 Read the exam task. What healthy snacks might be provided at a college? What prices would you pay for them?

> Your college recently introduced a snack bar with the aim of offering students healthy snacks during break times. You have conducted a student survey to gauge opinions of the new service. In the survey, you asked about the quality and variety of the snacks available, and their value for money.
>
> Write a report for the catering manager of the snack bar briefly explaining how you conducted the survey, describing the feedback you received, and suggesting improvements to the service.

2 Read the task again. Which points should you address in your report? Make brief notes about each one.

3 Read the report. Write a heading for paragraphs 1–5.

> **1** _____
> The purpose of this report is to provide the results of a student survey about the new snack bar and offer suggestions for improvements.
>
> **2** _____
> A group of 50 randomly-selected students were emailed the following five open questions about the snack bar: 1 Do you like the variety of snacks available? 2 What other snacks would you like to see? 3 Are the snacks good quality? 4 Are they well-priced? 5 Do have you have any suggested improvements?
>
> **3** _____
> The overwhelming majority of respondents reported that although there was a range of good-quality, healthy snacks available, certain items were missing. There were ª _____ small fruits like berries, or raw vegetables. While it was felt that most items were priced well, some, such as nuts, were more expensive than students expected, and currently ᵇ _____ of them are purchasing these. There was also high demand for opening hours to be extended to include lunchtimes, in addition to morning and afternoon breaks.
>
> **4** _____
> Based on the survey results, the following recommendations are made: widen snack choices to include items such as cherries and carrot sticks and open at midday to provide the opportunity to purchase snacks during the lunch period, ᶜ _____ this cannot be agreed with the principal.
>
> **5** _____
> To sum up, students are generally pleased to have the chance to buy healthy snacks during the school day, and ᵈ _____ the above suggestions are implemented, are happy to continue visiting the snack bar.

4 Complete the gaps a–d in the report with the words in the box. You do not need to use all the words.

> providing supposing unless
> neither no not none nor

EXAM TIP

Reports contain individual sections with appropriate headings. Make notes about what to include in each section and what the headings will be before you start writing.

✓ EXAM TASK WRITING PART 2

> You have just had a 'Health Week' at college, which involved students attending a series of events related to health, including presentations and workshops.
>
> Your college principal has asked you to write a report about the Health Week. You report should briefly describe the events that took place, explain what the benefits to students were of attending the events, and make suggestions for improvements for a similar event in the future.
>
> Write your **report**.

5 Write your answer in 220–260 words in an appropriate style.

SELF-EVALUATION

Check your writing:

Content: Have you included all three points that you were asked to address in your report? ☹ 🙁 😐 🙂

Communication: Is the target reader fully informed of your ideas and reasons for them? ☹ 🙁 😐 🙂

Organisation: Have your organised your report into appropriate sections? ☹ 🙁 😐 🙂

Language: Have you used a range of vocabulary and grammatical structures accurately? ☹ 🙁 😐 🙂

PREVENT, PROMOTE, PROTECT

1 GETTING STARTED

vaccine (n) /ˈvæksiːn/ a substance you put into the body to help it fight a disease

vaccination (n) /ˌvæksɪˈneɪʃən/ the process of giving someone a vaccine

What were three interesting or surprising facts you learned from the article on Student's Book page 104?

_____
_____
_____

2 THINK

How have vaccines helped?	
Challenges of vaccinating:	
Encouraging a healthy lifestyle:	

TIP When brainstorming, think about the best way to organise your ideas. You might like to make mind maps or lists, you might prefer to write by hand, or you might find typing is better. Don't forget, your brainstorm ideas are just for you, so it doesn't matter if they're messy!

3 EXPLORE

My group is: _____

The aspect of global health we will explore is: _____

What we already know:
_____
_____
_____

What we want to find out:
_____
_____
_____
_____

TIP Divide up your research in your group and make sure everyone knows which part they are responsible for. Set yourself a deadline and decide how you will share your research.

EXPLORING SUSTAINABILITY 1

4 DEVELOP

What are the most important points from your research?

- _____
- _____
- _____
- _____

Do you think the area of health you researched has got better or worse? _____

What evidence do you have for this? _____

What are your predictions for this area of health for the future? _____

Your Factsheet

Title: _____

Sub-headings	
Info to include	
Who will write it?	

> **TIP** Decide what to include in each section of the presentation so you don't repeat information. You should also decide who will be responsible for editing and design.

> **TIP** Don't just read your factsheet! Think about how to explain and expand on your ideas for the audience.

5 PRESENT

Plan who will be responsible for each part of presenting your factsheet:

_____
_____

Make notes on how to start and end the presentation:

Start: _____
End: _____

After the presentation …

Did you feel confident and prepared for the presentation? _____

What did you think your group did well in the presentation? _____

What areas do you want to work on next time?
_____
_____

SELF-EVALUATION

I can …

- innovate and problem solve to come up with solutions and recommendations. ○
- research and collect and record data related to a research topic. ○
- consider the welfare of present and future generations. ○
- create a factsheet to display research findings. ○

UNIT 2 BODY POSITIVE

UNIT 3 FOOD FOR THOUGHT

VOCABULARY
DESCRIBING FOOD

1 **Sort the adjectives in the box into three groups: positive, negative and neutral.**

> bland chewy crispy crunchy greasy
> inedible moreish mouthwatering
> savoury stale tender unappetising

2 **Write at least two types of food for each of the adjectives in Exercise 1.**

3 >>> STRETCH! **Complete the restaurant reviews with the words from Exercise 1. Use each word only once.**

★★★★★ Write a review

I booked this restaurant for my girlfriend's birthday last week. We weren't disappointed! I ordered a steak that was the most ¹ _____ I've ever tried. It was served with ² _____ chips which were really ³ _____. I couldn't stop eating them! It also had a salad of fresh, ⁴ _____ lettuce with a delicious dressing. For dessert, we shared a brownie with ice cream. It was absolutely ⁵ _____, probably the best one I've ever eaten. I don't eat dessert often as I prefer ⁶ _____ food, but I'll definitely order it again.

★★★★★

This was my first time at this restaurant and I won't be returning! First, they gave us some old bread that was ⁷ _____. Then I ordered the seafood pasta, but it had no flavour; it was really ⁸ _____, and the prawns were tough and ⁹ _____. It had obviously been cooked for too long. It also looked really ¹⁰ _____, all grey and sad. We ordered some chips instead, but they were so ¹¹ _____ and covered in oil that they were ¹² _____! Disappointing.

EXAM TIP

Read the text first to gain an understanding of the topic. Then complete the gaps with the appropriate word.

READING AND USE OF ENGLISH

✓ **EXAM TASK** READING AND USE OF ENGLISH PART 1

1 **For questions 1–8, read the text below and decide which answer (A, B, C, or D) best fits each gap. There is an example at the beginning (0).**

The earliest bread

Bread has been one of the most **(0)** _widely_ consumed staple foods in the world since prehistoric times. The earliest archaeological evidence of bread dates back 23,000 years and **(1)** ____ that hunter-gatherers collected grains and used stone slabs to **(2)** ____ them into flour.

It's likely that these earliest breads **(3)** ____ only crushed grain and water, and this mixture was placed on heated stones and baked in hot ashes. These were flatbreads, **(4)** ____ made of corn, barley and millet. Such grains lack the **(5)** ____ required to make raised breads, but they have **(6)** ____ as a speciality across much of the Middle East, Asia and Africa.

Scholars **(7)** ____ the ancient Egyptians with the discovery of fermentation: leaving dough mixture to form gas bubbles which expand and lighten bread. It was probably an **(8)** ____ discovery that happened when a batch of dough bound for baking was left forgotten. Fortunately, this oversight led to the development of the mouthwatering breads that we recognise today.

0 A broadly   B highly
   C widely   D largely
1 A exposes   B informs
   C discloses   D reveals
2 A rub   B grind
   C scrape   D grate
3 A consisted   B composed
   C comprised   D constituted
4 A principally   B fundamentally
   C significantly D extensively
5 A traits   B properties
   C aspects   D factors
6 A extended   B sustained
   C endured   D prolonged
7 A recognise   B acknowledge
   C regard   D credit
8 A accidental   B aimless
   C involuntary   D unthinking

READING

EXAM TASK READING AND USE OF ENGLISH PART 6

1 You are going to read four extracts from articles in which food critics give their views on eating out and dining in. For questions 1–4, choose from the food critics A–D. The critics may be chosen more than once.

EAT OUT or dine in?

Four food critics discuss the merits of eating out versus dining in.

A Most people eat at the home the majority of the time and treat themselves to a restaurant meal every once in a while. In many places, sky-rocketing prices mean going to a restaurant may soon be completely out of reach for many of us, and what a shame that would be. It's difficult to capture the ambience, the vibrant life, of a restaurant in your own kitchen. Unless you're a genius in the kitchen with plenty of time to spare for conjuring up each daily dinner, which, let's face it, is unlikely, then most of your meals will be fairly repetitive, with quick, easy 'go-tos' that can be rustled up in minutes after a long day at work. Eating out provides a welcome break from routine ingredients and flavours and is a chance to give our tastebuds something different that we might otherwise never taste.

B It's never been easier to eat out with a bunch of people all with different food preferences. Unless opting for a specific cuisine, menus cater for a range of tastes: the same restaurant will offer fish, vegetarian, spicy and bland options. This adds to the feeling of being looked after, a sense of comfort and care in softly lit surroundings, much like we have in our own private spaces. And those who may previously have struggled with eating out because of allergies or intolerances, amongst other things, can now confidently and safely go to a restaurant and order food in the full knowledge of its ingredients, and they won't have to pay more for the pleasure. We generally aren't master chefs, and tend to throw a meal together with little thought. Now and again, it's nice to see the results of a true professional's skills on the table in front of us.

C Eating out has become a luxury few can afford. That's the case in local pizzerias and cafés, never mind top-rate establishments with celebrity chefs presiding over the kitchen. It's a pity it's come to this if, like me, your usual *modus operandi* is shoving a pre-prepared supermarket dinner in the oven. We may forever miss out on the finer things chefs have to offer – dishes requiring ingredients we've never heard of, combined with cooking techniques that deliver the wow factor. And for anyone who's mindful of what they're eating, preferring whole foods with no additives that might cause reactions, they can dine in the knowledge that chefs can clarify exactly what's in a dish. Eating out isn't just about food, though: it's about sharing the experience – with our own party and those around us. There's an air of excitement about it that's almost impossible to carry over into our own dining rooms.

D The wealth of 'how-to' websites and cooking programmes has increased our desire to become rulers of our own kitchens, and there's been a swing towards restaurant-style cooking at home. You'd think this would make it a cheaper option than eating out, now hugely overpriced, but this isn't necessarily the case: fancy food requires fancy ingredients. This means digging deep into our wallets, but at least our dishes will feel luxurious, despite their complexity and the required skill level entailing longer periods at the cooker. Dining in is the new eating out. No need to dress up, stomp about in bad weather, or struggle to hear your companions over the din of the restaurant. Home's cosier. Plus, we know exactly what's in the food and can work round dietary requirements. This isn't to say restaurants no longer have value – sometimes you just want a plateful of the local restaurant's signature dish.

Which food critic

has a different opinion from the others about the way in which many people cook on a daily basis?	1
shares A's view on how easy it is to recreate the atmosphere of restaurants at home?	2
shares B's view on whether there are health risks involved in eating out?	3
expresses a different view from A on the cost of eating out?	4

GRAMMAR

LINKING IDEAS: RELATIVE CLAUSES

1 Match the sentence halves, then add the missing word.

1 Do you know anyone
2 That Mexican restaurant is the one
3 My mum,
4 The salad has got walnuts in,
5 He wanted to cook something
6 That chef has just got a new TV programme,

a _____ is normally great at cooking, made a curry that was inedible.
b _____ is set in his restaurant.
c _____ we went to last month.
d _____ I am allergic to.
e _____ could cater for my party?
f _____ was healthier than junk food.

2 Complete the text with *who*, *which* or *that*. Write X if you do not need a word. There may be more than one possible answer.

| HOME | CONTACT | Search... |

This month, in an attempt to be healthier and cut down on food waste, I've been trying a new app ¹_____ helps you to find recipes quickly and easily. The app, ²_____ was developed by a nutritionist and a chef, analyses the food ³_____ you have and suggests recipes you could make using it.

To use it, you input all the food in your fridge and cupboard, entering the 'use-by' dates so you can use the oldest food, or food ⁴_____ needs using the soonest, first. This is great for people like me ⁵_____ are often finding old food in the fridge ⁶_____ I then have to throw away! The app also provides a list of recipes ⁷_____ you could make with the food that you have. It's really useful for planning meals and it's saved me money because I'm wasting less food. My sister, ⁸_____ also loves cooking, has downloaded it too, and is really enjoying the recipes.

LINKING IDEAS: PARTICIPLE CLAUSES

3 Complete the paragraph with the correct form of the verbs in the box.

cook   have   live   open
prepare   waste   work   worry

When I was a private chef ¹_____ in Hong Kong, I had to make lots of weird and wonderful meals for my rich clients. One couple ordered elaborate meals every night. ²_____ made the meal, I then had to watch as they barely ate any of it! ³_____ food is something I hate, so that was difficult. Another client only ate food ⁴_____ with no fat at all; so no oil, butter, etc. ⁵_____ that I wouldn't follow this rule, they would often watch me cook. ⁶_____ every day while they were watching me was stressful! After ⁷_____ as a private chef for three years, I decided I wanted to cook the food I love. ⁸_____ my own restaurant last year was the best thing I have ever done.

LINKING IDEAS: RELATIVE PRONOUNS WITH PREPOSITIONS

4 Complete the sentences with the correct preposition.

1 The seafront restaurants, all _____ which specialise in fish, are quite expensive.
2 Trainee chefs, _____ whom cooking should be a joy, are often very stressed.
3 The café _____ which my friend works is looking for more waiting staff.
4 Jacques found two recipes for carrot cake, neither _____ which looked easy.
5 The shopkeeper, _____ whom we had argued before, tried to overcharge us.
6 I asked all my relatives, none _____ whom had seen my grandmother's recipe book.
7 They live in a second floor flat, _____ which is a Chinese takeaway.
8 He's studying nutrition, _____ which I know very little.

5 Complete the text with the correct options, A, B or C.

Having a meal should be a time when you are happy and relaxed, perhaps enjoying the company of people with ¹ ___ you live. But for those with coeliac disease, having a meal can be followed by painful and unpleasant symptoms.

Coeliac disease is a condition in ² ___ the immune system is affected. The disease causes a reaction in the immune system ³ ___ the body attacks the substances inside gluten, thinking they are a threat to the body. Sufferers of coeliac disease, all ⁴ ___ have to avoid wheat, barley and rye, can have symptoms such as stomach ache, diarrhoea and tiredness.

Currently there is no cure for coeliac disease, so people with the disease have to be careful about the food they buy and the restaurants ⁵ ___ which they eat. Many supermarkets now have large sections ⁶ ___ gluten-free foods can be bought. However, eating out can be more difficult. Most cities have hundreds of restaurants, only ⁷ ___ of which will cater for coeliacs. Coeliacs, ⁸ ___ whom get used to not being able to eat out, have to check ingredients very carefully when eating away from home.

1	A who	B that	C whom
2	A when	B which	C whose
3	A when	B whereby	C of which
4	A of whom	B of whose	C of them
5	A where	B with	C in
6	A whereby	B where	C whose
7	A a few	B all	C none
8	A many of	B neither of	C of

6 Complete the sentences with *where*, *when*, *whose* or *whereby* and your own ideas.

1 There's a restaurant in my town _____.
2 Having dinner is a time _____.
3 _____ is someone _____.
4 _____ taught me a trick in the kitchen _____.

VOCABULARY

PHRASAL VERBS: FOOD AND DRINK

1 Complete the sentences with the correct form of the phrasal verbs in the box. You may need to add the subject.

> cut out   force down   gulp down
> pick at   polish off   tuck into   warm up
> wash down   whip up   wolf down

1 My friend decided she eats too much sugar, so has completely _____ fizzy drinks.
2 Every time I go to see my grandad, he always _____ an amazing meal for me.
3 Whenever there is chocolate in the house, my brother _____ before anyone else gets any.
4 I was really late this morning, so I had to _____ my toast and _____ my coffee in five minutes.
5 We _____ our meal with some freshly squeezed orange juice.
6 That burger was disgusting, but I _____ because I didn't want to offend my friend.
7 I'm just going to _____ some of the soup I made yesterday. Want any?
8 My sister has the flu and has lost her appetite. She just _____ her food.
9 I was so hungry after our walk that I couldn't wait to _____ dinner.

2 Answer the questions for you.

1 What is something you always wolf down?
2 What is a snack you can whip up quickly?
3 What is a food you have to force down?
4 Do you pick at food or tuck into it?
5 Are there any foods you think you should cut out of your diet?

UNIT 3 FOOD FOR THOUGHT | 23

LISTENING

1 **You are going to listen to an interview about trends in cooking and eating, for example the use of equipment like air fryers. Can you think of any new food trends in your country?**

2 **Match the words and phrases 1–6 to the definitions a–f.**

  1 classic
  2 fad
  3 forage
  4 provenance
  5 signature dish
  6 zero waste

  a search for and collect food in the wild
  b using every part of something and throwing nothing away
  c the place of origin of something
  d a style, activity or interest that is popular only for a short time
  e traditional and high quality
  f a recipe that identifies a particular restaurant or chef

3 🔊 **3.1 Listen to the interview. Write the names of the major cooking and eating trends that are mentioned.**

EXAM TIP

Read the questions and options quickly and underline any key words or phrases before you listen. You may not hear exactly the same words in the recording, but you will hear the same ideas.

4 **Read the questions in the exam task and underline the key words.**

EXAM TASK — LISTENING PART 3

5 🔊 **3.1 You will hear an interview in which two food journalists called Marta Gonzalez and Richie Sanders are talking about trends in cooking and eating. For questions 1–6, choose the answer (A, B, C or D) which fits best according to what you hear.**

1 Marta believes that 'zero waste' cooking
  A is a concept that is being most strongly promoted in restaurants.
  B is becoming established as a cheaper alternative to traditional cooking.
  C is driven by a desire to look as though we're doing the right thing.
  D is an activity that previous generations did as a matter of course.

2 Richie says that dishes that are promoted as 'new'
  A often fail to appeal to the ordinary customer.
  B tend to be things that we recognise in some way.
  C suggest that chefs aren't as creative as they pretend.
  D usually involve items few people would describe as food.

3 Marta thinks that consumers' desire to know where food comes from
  A has stemmed from attempts to eat a more balanced diet.
  B is sometimes taken advantage of by food manufacturers.
  C is related to people wanting to eat more sustainably.
  D has become a major focus of supermarkets.

4 How does Richie feel about superfoods?
  A sorry that the idea has proven to be a myth
  B pleased that they have become so easy to get hold of
  C surprised that he actually enjoys eating them
  D hopeful that they have done him some good

5 What do Marta and Richie agree about DJs in restaurants?
  A They should make every effort to create the right kind of mood.
  B They help to offer customers an original dining experience.
  C They are more suited to a particular style of restaurant.
  D They can help promote the restaurants in question.

6 When Marta is asked about the idea of 'restaurant-to-retail', she expresses
  A worry that customers may be being taken advantage of.
  B interest in the unusual nature of the products being sold.
  C surprise about the effect it is already having on consumers.
  D scepticism about whether what's on offer is genuinely appetising.

24 | UNIT 3 FOOD FOR THOUGHT

WRITING

A REVIEW

1 What topics in the box might you write about in a restaurant or café review? Why?

> atmosphere   service   food
> tableware (glass, knives, plates)
> location   organisation of the kitchen
> choice of food   prices   other guests

2 Which adjectives in the box might you use to describe each aspect in Exercise 1? You may choose more than one word.

> appalling   attentive   disappointing
> efficient   exceptional   extensive
> high-quality   inedible   lively   remote
> spectacular   steep   unappetising

3 Read the writing task below and the review. Think of a title for the review.

> Have you recently visited a food outlet that offers cuisine you've never tried before? If so, please send us a review.
>
> Tell us about the cuisine, how the outlet is geared towards its target customers, and why you would or would not recommend the outlet to other people of your age.

4 Complete gaps 1–6 in the review with *who*, *which*, *where* or *whose*.

EXAM TIP

Look at the exam task. Make notes about your answers to each question. Think about the order in which you will present the information, and include some descriptive language.

EXAM TASK WRITING PART 2

You see the following announcement on a website about food.

> **Reviews wanted**
>
> We want to know about our followers' most unusual dining experiences, such as eating at an exciting location.
>
> What was so unusual about the meal? Why do you think some people seek out interesting dining experiences?

Write your **review**.

5 Read the exam task. Write your answer in 220–260 words in an appropriate style.

6 **Communication** The style of communication needed in texts depends on what you are writing. For example, a report communicates data, and recommendations, while an email asks and answers questions. What type of information does a review need to communicate? Do you do this successfully in your review?

SELF-EVALUATION

Check your writing:

Content: Are the ideas and opinions in your review relevant and well supported? Have you answered all the questions? ☹ 😐 🙂 😃

Communication: Have you held the reader's attention throughout? ☹ 😐 🙂 😃

Organisation: Have you used a variety of cohesive devices and organised your review appropriately? ☹ 😐 🙂 😃

Language: Have you used a range of vocabulary and grammatical structures accurately? ☹ 😐 🙂 😃

★★★★★ I visited Olivia's cafe on Thursday afternoon. It caters for those with a gluten intolerance and it is also vegan. Unfortunately, the food – ¹_____ eventually turned up after a wait of 50 minutes – was bland and strangely greasy. My dish consisted of spinach and potatoes with spices and was rather unimaginative. It was also served at room temperature, ²_____ was a bit of a let-down.

First impressions were of a cosy interior, with benches and large tables ³_____ people could sit together. While it was clearly trying to appeal to the younger market and there was a welcoming atmosphere, it was considerably less comfortable than it initially appeared, and could have done with a fresh coat of paint. The music wasn't up-to-date, ⁴_____ was disappointing. However, being in the town centre meant the café had a lively buzz, and the waiting staff, ⁵_____ were clearly doing their best, were pleasant enough.

I wouldn't recommend Olivia's to people of my age. Although it is clearly aimed at a younger market, it needs to update its decor and lower prices for students ⁶_____ budgets do not stretch to expensive meals. I would give the place another chance in the future in case I caught them on a bad day, but will leave it a while before I do so.

PRESENTATION SKILLS

How do you feel about giving a presentation? Why?

1 USING A RANGE OF GESTURES AND BODY MOVEMENTS

Tick the mistakes you think you make when giving a presentation.

standing too still ☐ reading notes / avoiding eye contact ☐
moving too much ☐ using too many gestures ☐
not facing the audience ☐ using not enough or too many facial expressions ☐

Which of these things do you think you could improve? How could you do this?

_____
_____
_____
_____
_____
_____
_____

2 ORGANISING THE CONTENT AND STRUCTURE OF MY TALK

My presentation is about: _____

Make notes to organise your ideas
Introduction:
_____
_____

Main section:
_____
_____
_____

Conclusion:
_____
_____
_____

 TIP Remember to use words and phrases to signpost your talk (e.g. *first, now, finally,* etc). Add some useful vocabulary to your notes.

26 | UNIT 3 FOOD FOR THOUGHT

3 SPEAKING CONFIDENTLY AND ENGAGING THE AUDIENCE

ORACY 2

How can you make your presentation more interesting for the audience? Look at these ideas. Can you think of any more?

- Start with a question to the audience
- Start with an interesting or surprising fact
- Tell a joke or funny story (related to the topic!)
- Use props or pictures
- Ask for follow-up questions at the end

_____
_____
_____

Which of these ideas could you use in your presentation?

Three things I want feedback on:
- _____
- _____
- _____

Ask a friend to listen to you practise your presentation and make notes on these things.

As you listen, make notes on the points your partner asked you to focus on.

_____
_____
_____
_____

Reflections on the presentation

Things that went well:
_____

Things that could be improved:
_____

Techniques you used to engage the audience:
_____

Things you changed after feedback from your partner:
_____

SELF-EVALUATION

I can ...
- use a range of gestures and body movements during a presentation. ○
- organise the content and structure of a talk to convey meaning. ○
- speak confidently and engage an audience in different ways. ○

REVIEW 1 UNITS 1–3

GRAMMAR 1

1 Complete the sentences with the correct future form of the verb in brackets. Sometimes more than one answer is possible.

1. By the time I finish school, I _____ (spent) 12 years in education.
2. I can't call you at 6 pm because I _____ (be) on the bus then.
3. Are you _____ (go) the career day next week?
4. This time next week, we _____ (sit) our chemistry exam.
5. The meeting _____ (finish) after lunch.
6. I _____ (work) for five hours already by the time you start your shift.
7. I _____ (have) a video call with the whole project team at 3 pm today.

2 Choose the correct answers to complete the text.

Lightsense Engineering is ¹ *about to / bound to* reveal an exciting new training programme. It is ² *on the verge of / set to* completely change the way we help our employees develop by having a range of online courses and training programmes you can enrol on in order to develop your knowledge. There are courses on first aid, using AI, design, health and safety and much more. You ³ *are set to / are bound to* find something that will interest you. The website ⁴ *is about to / is to be* the central place for all our online training. We ⁵ *are also on the verge of / are also to* sending out information about how to record your professional development online.

3 Find and correct six errors in the text.

> ⟨ Inbox   2 Messages   ⌃ ⌄
>
> Hi Julian,
>
> Congratulations on finishing school! You're on the verge a whole new chapter in your life. I heard you'll be going to work with Uncle Lonnie at the garage next month? I hope you will learned how to fix my car by the next time I see you! And then your mum said you're going to travelling in Asia for a while. You're bound of have fun there! Hopefully, by the time you return, you are going to have a better idea of what you want to do next in your life. I'm also going to Asia soon. In fact, this time next week, I am lying on a beach in Thailand!
>
> Love,
>
> Aunt Joanie

VOCABULARY 1

1 Complete the paragraph with the correct form of the words in the box. There may be more than one possible answer.

> beyond circumstances dramatic
> fresh gradual remain start stay
> steady sweeping times undergo

There are many predictions about how the world of work will change in the next 50 to 100 years. Some people think things will change ¹_____ recognition, but others think that we will see more of a slow and ²_____ shift. One thing that is predicted to bring about a ³_____ change is the use of AI. Some people even predict that this could lead to some industries ⁴_____ a complete transformation. Even jobs like teaching, which have largely ⁵_____ the same for hundreds of years, might need to move with the ⁶_____ due to an increased use of virtual reality in the classroom. Another area that is already experiencing a ⁷_____ change in many countries is the idea of flexible or remote working. Will we see ⁸_____ changes made to where and how we work in the future, or will things largely ⁹_____ unchanged? No one can predict the future, but it seems clear that workers who don't adapt to changing ¹⁰_____ may well be left behind, or perhaps it will be time for them to make a ¹¹_____ start and retrain so they can ¹²_____ from scratch in a new industry.

2 Match the verbs to the prepositions to make phrasal verbs from Unit 1.

1. rake
2. fall
3. shake
4. plug
5. resort
6. do
7. head / lay
8. wipe

a up
b away with
c off
d out
e in
f to
g into
h away

28 | REVIEW 1

GRAMMAR 2

1 Complete the second sentence so that it has a similar meaning to the first, using word given.

1. I've never broken any of the bones in my body. **NONE**
   I've broken _____.
2. I felt so sick yesterday that I didn't eat any food at all. **WHATSOEVER**
   I felt so sick _____.
3. My friend and I don't like the new gym in town. **NOR**
   Neither my friend _____.
4. Running isn't better for you than playing tennis. **NO**
   Running is _____.
5. I've tried two different smoothies and they both tasted bad. **NEITHER**
   I've tried _____.
6. I don't like running with other people, but I do like running alone. **NOT**
   I like running alone, _____.

2 Complete the advert with the words in the box. Use each word only once.

> as long as   imagine   otherwise
> providing   supposing   were to

---

¹_____ there was a way to not only keep fit, but also learn how to protect yourself, make friends and become more confident? Sounds good, doesn't it? Well, if you ²_____ join our martial arts club, we can help you with all those things and more! ³_____ you're prepared to train hard, you'll be welcome in our classes. ⁴_____ , you can soon be fitter and be able to defend yourself! ⁵_____ that you're over the age of 16, you can enrol today.

Come to our open day on the 14th September, ⁶_____ visit our website for more information.

VOCABULARY 2

1 Complete the email with the correct form of the phrases in the box.

> bite your tongue   blow your mind
> breathe down someone's neck   get cold feet
> get something off your chest
> go over your head   have a change of heart
> make your blood boil   pick someone's brains
> twist someone's arm

< Inbox   2 Messages   ∧ ∨

Hi Lola,

Sorry to contact you so late, but I really need to ¹_____. I can't believe what happened in my tennis match today – it's really ²_____. I'm so angry! My coach has been ³_____ for months about improving my serve. Today, it was match point for me and, for once, I did a perfect serve! The umpire said it was OK, but the other player said it was out! She really tried to ⁴_____ the umpire's _____ into ⁵_____. Then the umpire said actually, she thought it was out! It ⁶_____ that she could just change her mind for no reason! Anyway, I lost the match and then the other player smiled and said, 'never mind, unlucky'! I really had to ⁷_____ not to say something to her! I thought about talking to the umpire afterwards, but I ⁸_____.

Anyway, next time I see you, it would be good to ⁹_____ about how to handle these sorts of situations. I tried to talk to my mum about it, but anything about tennis just ¹⁰_____!

Annika

2 Match the phrases 1–11 to the questions a–d. You can use the phrases more than once.

1. boost mental health
2. suffer from a chronic disease
3. maintain a positive attitude
4. get plenty of exercise
5. respond to treatment
6. have adverse side effects
7. reduce stress levels
8. avoid processed foods
9. build up your strength
10. require medical attention
11. be in poor health

Which of these are …

a. reasons to visit a doctor? _____
b. things to do to be healthier? _____
c. things you might do need to do when recovering from an illness? _____
d. things that can happen after taking medication? _____

REVIEW 1 | 29

REVIEW 1 UNITS 1–3

GRAMMAR 3

1 Combine the two sentences using a relative clause.

1 My aunt always gives us fresh fruit and vegetables. She grows a lot of food.
2 The Korean restaurant is closing. You like it.
3 The flour went out of date five years ago. It was in the back of the cupboard.
4 Daniella gave me a recipe for tamales. It was very complicated.
5 We talked to a farmer. He told us the best ingredients to buy at this time of year.
6 Dinner is going to be a chicken stew. It will be at 8 o'clock.

2 Choose the correct answers to complete the text.

Crisps are a snack that are ¹ *loving / loved* and ² *eating / eaten* around the world, but how they were invented? Apparently a rich boat owner, ³ *having / had* his dinner at a New York restaurant in 1853, complained that the chips were too thick. ⁴ *Sending / Sent* the dish back to the kitchen, he asked for the potatoes to be changed. ⁵ *Intending / Intended* to insult the diner, the chef sliced the potatoes as thin as he could and fried them until they were brown, thereby ⁶ *creating / created* the well-loved potato crisp.

Unfortunately, the story is just that. Nobody really knows when this snack ⁷ *selling / sold* around the world was invented, although a recipe for crisps was published in a British cookbook in 1817.

SELF-ASSESSMENT!

3 Look back at your work in Units 1–3.

☐ talking about the future
☐ *no, not, none, neither* and *nor*
☐ conditional concepts
☐ linking ideas

1 Tick ✓ the area of grammar that you feel most confident about.
2 Circle the area of grammar that you need to work on more.
3 Underline the area of grammar that you think you will use most in future.

VOCABULARY 3

1 Complete the sentences with the words in the box.

> bland chewy crispy crunchy greasy
> inedible moreish mouthwatering
> savoury stale tender unappetising

1 The sweets were so _____ they got stuck in my teeth, but also so _____ I couldn't stop eating them.
2 The last time I had fast food, the burger was _____ and the bread was _____! I like food that is less _____ and has more flavour.
3 I prefer _____ food to sweet. There's nothing better than _____ chips or a packet of _____ crisps.
4 That steak was amazing! It was so soft and _____ and absolutely _____.
5 The food at that café was disgusting. Not only did it look _____, it wasn't cooked properly so was completely _____.

2 Complete the paragraph with the correct prepositions.

For a few days before a triathlon, I try to cut ¹ _____ most fibre, but tuck ² _____ a lot of carbohydrates like pasta. Then, about an hour before the race, I polish ³ _____ a big bowl of porridge and a banana to give me energy for the swim. After that, I normally feel a bit ill, but force ⁴ _____ an energy bar on my bike. I can also gulp ⁵ _____ water while riding. I'll have another energy bar, washed ⁶ _____ with an energy drink, an hour later.

After the race, I eat something that I can warm ⁷ _____ quickly. Often I'm not that hungry so I just pick ⁸ _____ it. At home, my parents whip ⁹ _____ a meal for me, which I always wolf ¹⁰ _____ gratefully!

SELF-ASSESSMENT!

3 Look back at your work in Units 1–3.

☐ expressing change
☐ phrasal verbs
☐ body idioms
☐ health collocations
☐ describing food
☐ phrasal verbs: food and drink

1 Tick ✓ the vocabulary group that you enjoyed learning about the most.
2 Circle the vocabulary group that you need to work on more.
3 Underline the vocabulary group that you think you will use most in future.

VOCABULARY REFERENCE 1-3

UNIT 1

adapt to changing circumstances change as other things change
bring about a dramatic change alter something greatly
change beyond recognition become completely different
experience a gradual change change little by little
make a fresh start start over
make sweeping changes alter things greatly
move with the times change to stay up to date
remain unchanged stay the same
see a slow but steady shift change slowly over time
start again from scratch start again from the beginning
stay the same not change
undergo a complete transformation change completely
do away with get rid of something
fall into start doing something without intending to
head off start a journey
lay off stop employing someone, usually because there is no more work for them
plug away work hard for a long time
rake in earn a large amount of money
resort to do something you don't want to because there is no other way of achieving it
shake up make extensive changes to
wipe out eliminate or destroy completely

UNIT 2

bite your tongue force yourself not to say something
blow your mind amaze and excite you
breathe down someone's neck stay close to someone, watching everything they do
get cold feet become too nervous to do something
get something off your chest tell someone about something that you've been worrying about
go over your head be too difficult or strange to understand
have a change of heart change how you feel about something
make your blood boil make you extremely angry
pick someone's brains ask someone who knows a lot about a subject for information or their opinion
twist someone's arm persuade someone to do something they do not want to do

avoid processed foods try to eat fresh food
be in poor health be generally unwell
boost mental health improve the condition of your mind
build up your strength increase your health, especially after an illness
get plenty of exercise do lots of physical activity
have adverse side effects react badly to drugs or medical treatment alongside the effect that was intended
maintain a positive attitude stay full of hope or confidence
reduce stress levels feel less worried or anxious
require medical attention need to see a doctor
respond to treatment have a positive reaction to medicine or other cures
suffer from a chronic disease have a disease that continues for a long time

UNIT 3

bland not having a strong taste or any flavour
chewy needing to be chewed a lot
crispy hard enough to be broken easily
crunchy making a short, loud noise when you eat it
greasy covered with fat or oil
inedible not suitable for eating
moreish having a pleasant taste and making you want to eat more
mouthwatering looking as if it will taste good
savoury salty or spicy and not sweet in taste
stale old and not fresh
tender easy to cut or chew
unappetising not looking or smelling appealing
cut out stop eating or drinking something to improve your health
force down make yourself eat something
gulp down drink something quickly
pick at eat a small amount of food without enjoying it
polish off finish eating something quickly and easily
tuck into start eating something eagerly
warm up heat food that has already been cooked
wash down eat food or swallow medicine with a drink
whip up make food or a meal quickly and easily
wolf down eat something very quickly

DIGITAL CLASSROOM
PRACTICE EXTRA UNITS 1-3

UNIT 4 AMONG FRIENDS

VOCABULARY

FRIENDSHIP

1 Match 1–10 to a–j to make phrases.

1	bear	a	and downs
2	drift	b	your own company
3	enjoy	c	up a friendship
4	go	d	a grudge
5	ups	e	you up the wrong way
6	hit	f	someone behind their back
7	a shoulder	g	it off
8	rub	h	apart
9	strike	i	to cry on
10	talk about	j	back a long way

2 Complete the sentences with the correct form of a phrase in Exercise 1. Use each phrase once.

1 I've known Jimmy since we were babies. We really _____.

2 We used to be good friends, but we've _____ over the years.

3 My sister and I have had our _____ but, at the end of the day, she's family.

4 My friend and I _____ immediately on our first day of school.

5 I thought he was my friend, but then I heard he had been _____!

6 I've never got on with Frances. She just _____.

7 I'm quite a sociable person, but I also _____, too.

8 When my relationship finished last year, Frederica was there as _____.

9 My friend Omar and I fell out at my birthday party last year, but I'm trying not to _____ because we hang out with the same people.

10 I sometimes find it hard to _____ with new people.

READING

1 Why are friends so important in our lives? What different kinds of friendships do we have? What does each kind of friendship offer?

2 Read the article quickly. Does it mention any of the ideas you talked about in Exercise 1?

✓ EXAM TASK — READING AND USE OF ENGLISH PART 7

3 You are going to read an article about the importance of friendship. Six paragraphs have been removed from the article. Choose from the paragraphs A–G the one which fits each gap (1–6). There is one extra paragraph which you do not need to use.

A Casual interactions like these make a measurable difference to how we feel, inconsequential as they may seem at the time. They serve to lighten the mood and can even reveal things within us that we were previously unaware of.

B In fact, some of the longest-living people on Earth believe groups like those encountered in our free time or the office are key to leading not only a long life, but a fulfilling one. Residents of the Japanese island of Okinawa form strong alliances known as *moai* or 'meeting for a common goal'.

C The diversity and fresh perspectives that come with these particular groups help us grow and learn about ourselves and others, encouraging us to become well-rounded, tolerant, empathetic people. The more agreeable and understanding society is, the more we gain.

D It's an interesting thing to consider because each group has an impact on us, in however small a way. They may never become people we go to in a crisis, but still help shape our lives.

E Having negative feelings of this kind is what leads many of us to narrow down our social circles as we age, partly due to time constraints, but also because we're more established in life and become more discerning in our choices.

F We need every type, regardless of their place on the friendship continuum. They offer us an important sense of community, help create our identity, improve our life satisfaction, and even offer longevity: more social contact means a longer life expectancy.

G And we should make every effort too. We can start by looking toward our own friendships, and making efforts to maintain them. But only, that is, if they are mutually beneficial, satisfying and worthy of these efforts.

What friendship means to us

Psychologists classify friends into seven groups: lifelong friends, best friends, close friends, social group friends, activity friends, convenience friends, and acquaintances. The labels speak for themselves: acquaintances are the people we say 'Hi' to in passing, have a casual chat with when we happen to be in the same space, but who lack closeness on any real level; whereas best friends, at the other end of the scale, are the ones with whom we share our innermost secrets, the ones we trust implicitly.

| 1 |

The last of these advantages, psychologists say, comes about because engagement with others gives us purpose. And this is across the board: being a member of a tight-knit work team who have a sense of camaraderie and shared goals is equally as beneficial to our mental well-being – which has a knock-on effect on our physical health – as sharing a pizza and gossip with our closest crew, or competing in our team on the football pitch at weekends.

| 2 |

These have the express purpose of providing support in various spheres of life: social, financial, health, and spiritual interests. It's believed that having access to encouraging, reassuring and protective communities increases lifespan. Indeed, the region has one of the highest concentrations of centenarians in the world. Its people have a sense of usefulness gained through engaging in things that give life meaning, like work and caring for others, and hold secrets to happiness that many of us could learn from.

| 3 |

Indeed, psychologists don't condone hanging on to friendships that are detrimental to us. Nor do they advocate forcing friendships with people we have nothing in common with. Quality matters more than quantity, but quantity does matter. The reason some friends never make it into our 'inner circle' is because we don't have enough in common or enough time to nurture the relationship. This doesn't mean 'middle' or 'peripheral' friends have nothing to offer us.

| 4 |

But how far do we need to take such mutual regard? Can one have 'too many' friends? Research indicates that most of us are content with two or three 'besties' and a wider circle of social friends with whom we choose to spend our precious leisure time. We don't all need the same number, but we do all need to feel that the number we have is 'just right'. Fewer, and there's a risk of isolation; more, and we risk becoming overwhelmed with the responsibility of trying to keep up with everyone.

| 5 |

Abandoning low-value friendships is of benefit to us psychologically, and the number of lifelong, best and close friends are the strongest predictors of our overall happiness. That said, a friendly greeting from a neighbour, a sincere 'How are you?' from the shopkeeper in a store we frequent, a bit of friendly banter in our weekly exercise class, and even a quick chat about the weather with other parents at the school gates, all play their part.

| 6 |

This could be anything from a dormant sense of humour to a kind heart. No matter who brought it to light, we leave the situation feeling a little bit better about ourselves and our place in life.

EXAM TIP

Consider the meaning of the removed paragraphs, then look for ideas which link with the paragraphs before and after the gap. There will be other clues to help you, for example words and phrases (*indeed*, *in fact*), reference pronouns (*this*, *these*, *they*) and lexical links (words and phrases).

GRAMMAR

COMPARATIVES AND SUPERLATIVES REVIEW

1 Choose the correct answers.

1. My friends and I always go to the shop next to the bowling alley because it has the *cutest / cuter* clothes.
2. I can speak more *honesty / honestly* with my sister now we're both at college.
3. When our friendship group went to different universities, it wasn't *harder as a time as / as hard a time as* we thought it would be, as we still met in the holidays.
4. It's *a great deal more / of greater* convenient to have a video call than to go around to my friend's house.
5. The internet means that people can be *as close as ever / closer as ever* to their family despite living miles apart.
6. We're *far more able / much abler* to make friends all over the world these days.
7. Jimi is *a funnier / the funniest* person I know!
8. My mum rings me *the most / more* often of all my family members.

2 Complete the text with one word in each gap.

Now is ¹_____ far the easiest time in history to stay in touch with your friends and family, no matter where they live. We can contact anyone in the world much ²_____ quickly than ever before. But does this level of communication make us more or ³_____ lonely? Many people would argue that now is as difficult a time ⁴_____ any to have close relationships. Perhaps spending too much time online has made it a ⁵_____ deal more challenging to relate to people in real life. Or maybe relationships are now stronger than ⁶_____ because you can contact people wherever you are. One thing is for certain, this generation is the ⁷_____ connected we have ever seen and being able to negotiate relationships both on and offline could be a ⁸_____ more important in the future.

3 Complete the sentences with a comparative adverb or adjective and your own ideas.

1. Something I am able to do much more _____ these days is _____.
2. My friend _____ is the _____ person I know.
3. I think life is a great deal _____ than _____.

COMPARATIVES AND SUPERLATIVES EXTENSION

4 Complete the text with a double comparative or a double comparative with *the*. Use the adjectives in the box. There may be more than one possible answer.

good   difficult   excited   friendly
hard   lost   old   shy   small   unusual

My mum works for the military, so we move around a lot and I start a new school every couple of years or so. When I was younger, it was an adventure, but ¹_____ I am, ²_____ it gets. I find it ³_____ to make new friends because people have already established their groups. I used to be a friendly and confident person, but I'm becoming ⁴_____ around other people.

One thing I have found is that ⁵_____ the school, ⁶_____ people seem to be. My current school is huge and I've found I just get ⁷_____ among a sea of people. Also, it's good to join clubs, ⁸_____, ⁹_____! I love anime films, so I joined a movie club and made my best friends there. And next year, I'm going to university and I'm getting ¹⁰_____ about the fact that everyone will be new there!

5 Read the results of a class survey about how people keep in touch and complete the sentences.

	Social media	Telephone calls	Text message	Video call
Students	100%	47%	65%	89%
Parents	86%	72%	80%	73%
Grandparents	32%	88%	45%	22%

1 Considerably more students use social media than _____.
2 The older people get, the more they _____.
3 Grandparents are nowhere near as likely to _____.
4 Grandparents _____ as students.
5 The younger people are, _____.

6 >>> STRETCH! Complete the second sentence so that it has a similar meaning to the first, using the word given.

1 My brother is a great deal better at sport than me. **SIGNIFICANTLY**
I am _____.
2 Making a video call is a better way to stay in touch than texting. **NEARLY**
Texting _____.
3 Writing to my aunt wasn't as difficult a letter as I thought it would be. **A LOT**
Writing a letter _____.
4 She doesn't have anywhere near as many real friends as social media followers. **FAR**
She has _____.
5 My friend is a lot less funny than he thinks he is. **ANYWHERE**
My friend _____.
6 People are more and more likely to have friends in other countries these days. **INCREASINGLY**
These days _____.

VOCABULARY
PERSONALITY TRAITS

1 Read the descriptions. Then match the adjectives in the box to the people.

> cynical idealistic laid-back outgoing
> reserved sarcastic self-assured
> self-conscious sincere uptight

1 Antonio   6 Uncle Frank
2 Donna   7 Brother
3 Aunt Laura 8 Vinnie
4 Sister   9 Dad
5 Ben   10 Zahra

'My friends are all quite different. For example, Zahra can be funny, but I'm never sure if she means what she's saying or the exact opposite! Vinnie, on the other hand, is really sweet, but he can be quite quiet and hard to get to know. Then there's Donna. I think she'll be a CEO or something one day, and so does she! She's very confident in herself.'

'There are three people I really get on with. My Aunt Laura, who's really cheerful and optimistic and always thinks everything will turn out well. My neighbour Antonio, who I can trust because he always says what he believes. And, if I want a good night out, my cousin Ben! Everyone likes him – he's friendly and chatty and always has a good time.'

'I love my family, but I wish my dad would relax – he's always stressing about something! He's the complete opposite to his brother. My Uncle Frank's motto is "No worries!". I worry about my sister, too. She used to be really confident, but as she's got older she's become more concerned about how she looks. And since my brother's been working in finance, he doesn't trust people as much. He says everyone just cares about themselves."

2 Mark where you think you are on the lines. Write a sentence for each item, explaining your answer.

laid-back   ←——→   uptight
idealistic   ←——→   cynical
self-assured   ←——→   self-conscious
sarcastic   ←——→   sincere
outgoing   ←——→   reserved

UNIT 4 AMONG FRIENDS | 35

LISTENING

1 If you have a problem, who do you talk to and why? Write a sentence to explain your answer.

2 🔊 4.1 Listen to the conversation. Match the people in the box to the information.

> Ariana   Madelaine
> Mrs Weatherly   Naomi   Tilly

1 _____ : The girls' PE teacher
2 _____ : A member of the netball team that has been talking about someone behind her back
3 _____ : A school friend not on the netball team
4 _____ : An old friend also on the netball team
5 _____ : The captain of the netball team

3 🔊 4.1 Complete the sentences with the words in the box. Listen to the conversation again and check your answers.

> drama   get ahead   team
> tension   trouble   rumours

1 Tilly has picked up on some _____ .
2 Tilly thinks Naomi might be trying to cause _____ .
3 Ariana says she is sick of the _____ .
4 Tilly suggests that Ariana calls a _____ meeting to say she has heard some _____ .
5 Tilly tells Ariana not to _____ of herself by thinking about quitting.

4 🔊 4.1 Listen again. Answer the questions.

1 Why is Tilly surprised to hear about the problems between Ariana and Madelaine?
2 What has Madelaine supposedly said about Ariana?
3 Who is Naomi?
4 Does Tilly trust Naomi? Why? / Why not?
5 Why doesn't Ariana want to speak to her PE teacher?
6 What is Tilly's suggestion to solve the problem?
7 What does Tilly think will happen if they don't solve the problem?
8 What does Ariana threaten to do?

5 What do you think Ariana should do? Write her a message.

6 **Collaboration and Teamwork** Think about times you have worked in a team (e.g. sports teams, group work, musical groups). What have been the biggest challenges you have faced? What are the benefits of working in a team?

WRITING

AN INFORMAL EMAIL

1 Who might you write an informal email to? Choose from the options in the box.

an elderly family member
a colleague
a teacher
a best friend
an acquaintance
a boss

36 | UNIT 4 AMONG FRIENDS

2 Read the email in the writing task. Who wrote it? What do they want you to do?

> You have received an email from an English-speaking friend.
>
>> I'm writing an article for the college magazine about the importance of friends and I wondered whether you could help me?
>>
>> What do you think is the value of friendship in people's lives? Do you think it matters if we don't see our friends for long periods of time?
>>
>> Let me know what you think!

3 Read the model answer. What answers does the writer give to the questions?

> Hi!
>
> Thanks for emailing me. That sounds like an interesting article and I'd love to help.
>
> Friendships are very valuable, and many of us spend a great ¹_____ longer with our friends than we do with our families. In some cases, these people are far ²_____ open-minded and in tune with us than other people in our lives.
>
> Friends serve many purposes. First and foremost, they offer companionship and fun, but they also provide a shoulder to cry on, and advice and support when we're confused, upset or afraid. It's reciprocal, of course: we offer the same things in return. Not every friend needs to be close, though. We may have casual acquaintances who we know far less well ³_____ those we share interests and hobbies with. And in turn, we see those people ⁴_____ nearly as often as our best friends. There are friends we see at the gym, art club or singing group; others we count as 'fun' friends we socialise regularly with; and then we have our 'inner circle', those we spend ⁵_____ far the most time with, during good times and bad.
>
> If we have friends that go back a long way, and who we have a lot in common with, it doesn't matter if there's a long gap between meeting up: it'll be like we only saw them yesterday. But for those friends we share only limited spheres of our lives with, the less we see of them, ⁶_____ harder the relationships may be to maintain.
>
> These are my thoughts on friendship – I hope they help!

4 Complete the email in Exercise 3 with one word in each gap.

EXAM TIP

Read the email carefully. There will be questions for you to answer in your reply. Make sure you answer these fully.

5 Look at the questions in the second paragraph of the exam task below. How might you answer these questions? Make notes.

EXAM TASK WRITING PART 2

> You have received an email from an English-speaking friend.
>
>> I'm doing a project at college about friendship and wondered whether you'd mind answering a couple of questions?
>>
>> What do you think is a manageable number of friends a person should have? How do you think our friendships change as we go through life?
>>
>> Thanks!
>
> Write your **email**.

6 Write your answer in 220–260 words in an appropriate style.

SELF-EVALUATION

Check your writing:

Content: Have you answered all the questions fully, giving reason for your ideas and opinions? ☹ ☹ 😐 🙂

Communication: Have you communicated your ideas effectively, so that the reader is fully informed? ☹ ☹ 😐 🙂

Organisation: Is your email well-organised, with a range of cohesive devices? ☹ ☹ 😐 🙂

Language: Have you used a range of vocabulary and grammatical structures accurately? ☹ ☹ 😐 🙂

ARE YOU BIASED? PROBABLY!

1 GETTING STARTED

bias (n) /baɪəs/ being unfairly for or against a person or thing because of personal opinions

biased (adj) /baɪəst/ unreasonably liking or disliking someone or something because of personal opinions

What do you think about the quote *Appearances are often deceiving*? Can you think of any examples of this?

_____

What do you think people who saw you for the first time would think?

_____

Would they be right?

_____

2 THINK

Unconscious bias at school

TIP Think about your own experiences, experiences of friends and classmates. Try to write down as many ideas as you can – you can choose the best ones later.

3 EXPLORE

My group is: _____.

_____ will research examples of unconscious bias.

Notes: _____
_____

_____ will research practical solutions to unconscious bias.

Notes: _____
_____

TIP Make sure you keep a record of where you find your information so you can use it for references later.

UNIT 4 AMONG FRIENDS

4 DEVELOP

EXPLORING SUSTAINABILITY 2

Share your research and make notes in the table.

Priority No.	Bias (Summary)	Suggested actions	How will this improve things?

TIP You might not have the space in your letter to write about all your ideas. Select the two or three that are the most relevant to your school, or would have the biggest impact.

5 PRESENT

TIP Make sure you keep a record of where you find your information so you can use it for references later.

Use the checklist to check your letter:

- Have you started the letter appropriately? ☐
- Is your letter written in formal style? ☐
- Have you divided the letter into paragraphs? ☐
- Have you introduced the subject of your letter clearly? ☐
- Have you clearly explained what you want the headteacher to do? ☐
- Is your letter positive and does it explain how things will be improved? ☐
- Have you finished the letter appropriately? ☐
- Have you checked your spelling, punctuation and grammar? ☐
- Is your letter clear and easy to read? (Remember it will be displayed.) ☐

How will you present your letter? Make some notes:

Introduction: _____

Extra points you want to explain: _____

Conclusion: _____

SELF-EVALUATION

I can ...
- understand how beliefs and values contribute to sustainable behaviours. ○
- critically analyse the pros and cons of anonymous grading. ○
- organise issues and solutions in terms of priority. ○
- generate support for action through effective communication. ○
- summarise research in a letter. ○

UNIT 5 TIME OUT

VOCABULARY

EXPRESSIONS ABOUT TIME

1 **Replace the words in bold with the correct form of an expression in the box.**

> behind the times   call it a day   for good
> for the time being   have time on your hands
> in a flash   in the nick of time   kill time
> lose track of time   move with the times
> on the spur of the moment
> once in a blue moon

1 I only go to the cinema **very occasionally**. _____

2 If you **have any spare time** tomorrow, can you help me move my desk? _____

3 I was so busy talking to my friend that I **didn't realise the time**. _____

4 I think I'm going to give up ballet **completely**. I just don't have the time for it anymore. _____

5 Last weekend we just woke up and decided to take a train to the city **without planning it at all**. _____

6 Our family business really needs to **be modern** and start using social media. _____

2 **Complete the sentences with the expressions in the box that you did not use in Exercise 1.**

1 I'm tired so I'm going to _____ now and finish cleaning my room tomorrow.

2 I got there one minute before my train left. I was just _____!

3 I think _____, I'm going to continue studying Arabic and then see how I feel next year.

4 My geography teacher is so _____. He doesn't even have a mobile phone!

5 The programme was so good that it seemed to be over _____.

6 I've got two hours before my dentist appointment, so I'm going to find something to do to _____ while I wait.

3 >>> STRETCH! **Complete the text messages with expressions from Exercise 1.**

← Online

> Have you got any time on ¹_____ today? I need some help!

> Well, I've been doing some work on my essay, but I think I'm going to ² _____ a day soon. What do you need?

> Well, on the ³ _____ of the moment I decided to have a bath, so I turned the water on but then I ⁴ _____ of time ... and, well the bath overflowed and the bathroom is a bit wet ...

> Oh, no! 😨

> It's not too bad. I got there just ⁵ _____ of time I think! But I need some help cleaning up the mess.

> OK, don't worry. I'll be there ⁶ _____ a flash!

> Thank you! If my parents find out, I think they'll stop my allowance _____ good! 😞

READING

1 **What do you think it means to procrastinate? Read the blog to find out. Are you a procrastinator?**

2 **Read the blog again. Are the statements true, false or not given? Correct the false statements.**

1 Cecilia is worried about her exams.
2 Cecilia had planned to study at the weekend.
3 She didn't do much work on Saturday.
4 Cecilia normally has a lazy day on Sundays.
5 Cecilia couldn't find out how the 'Pomodoro technique' got its name.
6 In the 'Pomodoro technique', you get a longer rest every two hours.
7 'Eat the frog' is a time management technique.
8 'Frogs' are hard things you need to get done.
9 Some of Cecilia's classmates have tried study timetables.
10 Cecilia is trying one of the techniques first.

3 Match the bold words and phrases in the blog to the definitions.

1. _____ : something you are currently working on
2. _____ : immediately
3. _____ : change your habits or behaviour to be better
4. _____ : very busy
5. _____ : become so interested in something that you lose track of time researching it
6. _____ : made especially for you

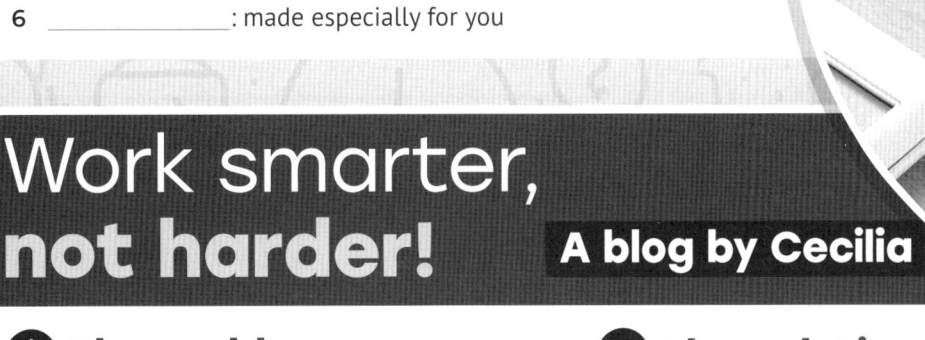

Work smarter, not harder!
A blog by Cecilia

⚠ The problem ...

This month is a really **hectic** one for me with three exams at the end of the month I need to revise for, a concert I need to practise for, and a first-aid course I'm going on ready to start my lifeguard job in the holidays.

So, I guess you're imagining I spent this weekend working really hard, right? Well, let's just say I intended to … I got up early on Saturday and set off for a run to wake myself up, but ended up bumping into my friend Tammy and chatting for about half an hour. Then I went home for a shower, dried my hair, did my make-up, chose some clothes … Finally, I sat down at my desk to study, but it was a mess and you know what they say – tidy desk, tidy mind! So, I decided to give it a clean, sharpen my pencils, arrange my books in colour order … I might have lost track of time a bit because the next thing I knew, it was lunchtime. After lunch my friend Lonnie called me, we chatted for a bit and then it was time for orchestra practice and dinner, and then I was tired so I thought I'd just call it a day and watch a film with my family.

But, you know, on Sunday I would **turn over a new leaf**, right? Well, let's just say I overslept a little bit. And then when I finally opened my laptop to work, I might have got a tiny bit distracted by watching videos on social media …

If you haven't guessed by now, I'm a bit of a procrastinator! I really need to find a way to keep my mind on the **task in hand**. So, on the spur of the moment I've decided that today, instead of focusing on my revision, I'm going to research the best ways to, umm, focus. Will this be just another distraction or the answer to all my problems?! Time will tell!

✓ The solutions ...?

The first technique I came across was the 'Pomodoro technique' (I'm not sure why it is named after the Italian word for *tomato*, but I'm trying not to get distracted so I'm not going to **go down a rabbit hole** looking for the reason). In this technique you set a timer for 25 minutes, really focus on whatever you need to get done until the timer goes off and then reward yourself with a five-minute break. After you've repeated this cycle four times, you get treated to a longer twenty- or thirty-minute break.

The second technique I found was called 'Eat the frog' (again, let's not get into the origin of the name here!). This is when you have a clear goal, write it down and then compile a list of things you need to do in order to achieve that goal, which you then organise in order of priority. The most important things are normally the most difficult (the frogs), so you do these first to get them out of the way.

Finally, I thought maybe I should try something that our teacher told us about which is to create a timetable where I break the day into one-hour slots and work out what I'm going to do in each one. Then I can colour-code it and cross off each hour as I finish. This way I can see **at a glance** exactly what I need to do when, and can work out in advance how everything will fit in.

⏩ What's next?

The plan for the rest of the week is to try to combine these ideas into a **bespoke** time management plan. I'll be making a timetable following the Pomodoro schedule and then making sure I timetable the tasks that are the most challenging for the beginning of the day. Will it work? Watch this space! I'll report back next week. For the time being though, I need to stop procrastinating and get on with some study!

4 💼 **Professional Development and Management** How do you manage your time? Which of the techniques from the blog do you think would be most useful for you to try?

GRAMMAR
INVERSION

1 Choose the correct answers to complete the sentences.

1 Rarely ___ people wearing watches these days.
   A you see   B do you see
   C you did see

2 ___ seen him, I would have given him a lift.
   A Had I   B Have I   C I had

3 ___ put the phone down when it rang again.
   A I hardly   B Had I hardly
   C Hardly had I

4 ___ waiting for my appointment for an hour, did I realise I had the wrong day.
   A Only after   B No sooner   C After

5 No sooner had I left the house ___ I realised I'd forgotten my keys.
   A when   B then   C than

6 Not only ___ sent reminders from the digital organiser, but it will connect to your emails too.
   A can you be   B you can be
   C can you

7 Had he ___ earlier, he wouldn't have got stuck in a traffic jam.
   A leave   B to leave   C left

8 ___ late again, I would go home.
   A When you were
   B Were you to be
   C You were being

MULTI-WORD VERBS

2 Find ten multi-word verbs in the paragraph.

I wish we could just do away with timetables because everyone has a different body clock. Some people like to get up early and others like to lie in. We could really shake up working and studying by allowing a more flexible approach to time. People wouldn't have to resort to starting work at a certain time each day. They could turn up to work or school when they were most productive and take time out when they needed to. As long as they don't let down anyone and hand in their work on time, then I don't see a problem with when things are done. If someone wants to stay up all night and work, then what's the problem?

3 Which three multi-word verbs in Exercise 2 are separable? Write them below.

_____
_____
_____

READING AND USE OF ENGLISH

EXAM TIP

The meaning of the second sentence must be as close as possible to the meaning of the first sentence, so make sure you read the first very carefully. Include the key word given without changing it in any way.

✓ EXAM TASK — READING AND USE OF ENGLISH PART 4

1 For questions 1–6, complete the second sentence so that it has a similar meaning to the first sentence, using the word given. Do not change the word given. You must use between three and six words, including the word given. There is an example (0).

0 Jana isn't interested in any job where she'd have to spend many hours at work each day.   **OF**
None ___*of the jobs*___ where she'd have to spend many hours at work every day interested Jana.

1 As soon as the match started, my phone began to ring.   **HAD**
No _____ off than my phone began to ring.

2 I've never met anyone anywhere near as judgemental as her.   **FAR**
She _____ judgemental person I've ever met.

3 What I mean by him not knowing a clock if he saw one is that he's always late.   **BY**
He wouldn't know a clock if he saw one, _____ he's always late.

4 I only felt relaxed again after getting changed.   **HAD**
Only once _____ feel relaxed again.

5 I don't seem to have any time management skills, and you don't either!   **NEITHER**
When it comes to time management skills, _____ seem to have any!

6 If I was made president of the club, I'd introduce new rules immediately.   **TO**
I'd introduce new rules immediately were _____ made president of the club.

42 | UNIT 5 TIME OUT

2 What is 'flow'? What activities might create a feeling of flow? Read the text in Exercise 3 and check your answers.

EXAM TIP

Read the whole text first for general understanding. As you read, think about what kind of word goes in each gap, e.g. a preposition, a pronoun, an article, a phrasal verb particle, a conjunction or an auxiliary verb.

✓ EXAM TASK — READING AND USE OF ENGLISH PART 2

3 For questions 1–8, read the text below and think of the word which best fits each gap. Use only one word in each gap. There is an example at the beginning (0).

Time speeds up when we're in 'flow'

What psychologists call being in a state of 'flow' **(0)** ___is___ what we might also know as being 'in the zone'. In other words, we're totally absorbed by the activity in **(1)** _____ we're engaged, and therefore oblivious to what's going on around us, and completely lose track **(2)** _____ time. We won't have heard the TV in the next room or have **(3)** _____ disturbed by the storm outside. Only when we're later informed of **(4)** _____ has gone on, do we realise we were 'missing' for a while. We'll wonder **(5)** _____ we could possibly have missed the torrential rain or the neighbour's dustbin flying down the road.

The phenomenon of flow creates a feeling of timelessness, **(6)** _____ in other words, time standing still. It comes about when we're **(7)** _____ involved in an activity that nothing around us matters. However, this only occurs when we're doing something we especially enjoy. Psychologists say flow helps us define who we are and makes us feel truly alive. It also serves **(8)** _____ give us a much-needed break from anything that's causing us stress in our lives.

VOCABULARY
MULTI-WORD VERBS: TIME

1 Complete the paragraph with the correct form of the multi-word verbs in the box.

> catch up on   bring forward   drag on   fit in
> fly by   hold up   lag behind   rush around

Do you want a chance to ¹_____ your studies?

Are you worried about ²_____ so want some extra support with your work?

Do you need help ³_____ all the work you need to complete?

Have you had a deadline ⁴_____ that you are now worried about meeting?

Our study days might be just the thing for you! Come and let our qualified tutors help you with your studies or revision. You don't have to worry about ⁵_____ anyone _____ as you can work at your own pace. We have a quiet study room, a meeting room for group work and a chill out room where you can have a break when your work starts to ⁶_____. You won't have to ⁷_____ trying to find the right books. We have a fully stocked library and access to many educational websites. We're sure time will ⁸_____ much quicker than struggling alone at home!

2 Answer the questions for you.
1. When do you find time drags on the most?
2. When do you find time flies by the fastest?
3. What is something you need to catch up on?
4. What is something you would like to do more but have trouble fitting in?

LISTENING

1. What do you think is meant by the phrase 'act your age'? Can you think of any examples of people that don't 'act their age'?

2. 🔊 5.1 Listen to the podcast and answer the questions.

   How old was/were …
   1. an Australian girl when she retired? _____
   2. a horse rider at the Olympics? _____
   3. two skateboarders at the Olympics? _____
   4. the oldest skydiver? _____
   5. the oldest graduate? _____
   6. the youngest graduate? _____

3. Match the words and phrases 1–5 to the definitions a–e.
   1. anti-wrinkle   4. dye
   2. conventions   5. pin someone down
   3. defy expectations

   a. don't do what people think you should do
   b. the usual or normal ways of behaving
   c. force someone to do something
   d. something that stops or reduces small lines on the skin
   e. change the colour of something by using a special liquid

4. 🔊 5.1 Listen to the podcast again. Write the words or phrases you hear related to time.

5. 🔊 5.1 Listen again. Answer the questions.
   1. What is the topic of the podcast?
   2. What are Nikki's mum's expectations of her?
   3. What are some examples of social expectations that have changed these days?
   4. Why does Rohan think people still want to look young?
   5. What reasons do the podcasters give for changing attitudes to age?
   6. What did the study in Germany reveal?

6. Answer the questions for you.
   1. Do you think it is important to 'act your age'? Why? / Why not?
   2. If you retired now, what would you do for the rest of your life?
   3. In your culture, at what age is it normal to:
      • get a job?   • have children?
      • get married?   • retire?
      Do you think you will follow these conventions? Why? / Why not?

WRITING

AN ESSAY

1. What do you think is the best way to spend free time? Why?

2. Read the writing task below. Then read the opinions in the task. Do you agree with them? Why? / Why not? What alternative arguments could you make for each of the opinions?

> In class, you have discussed the best ways to relax during the evenings.
>
> You have made the notes below:
>
> **What are the best ways to relax during the evenings?**
> • turning off electronic devices
> • listening to music
> • doing gentle exercise like yoga
>
> Some opinions expressed in the discussion:
>
> 'You can't switch off if you're still connected to the outside world.'
>
> 'Music can be relaxing, but it needs to be quiet and soothing.'
>
> 'Doing exercise makes some people more energetic rather than calming them down.'
>
> Write an essay in 220–260 words discussing **two** of the ways in your notes to relax during the evenings. You should **explain which of the ways is most beneficial to relaxation, giving reasons** to support your opinion.
>
> You may, if you wish, make use of the opinions expressed in the discussion, but you should use your own words as far as possible.

3 Read the essay. Which of the points does the writer discuss? What reasons do they give for their answers?

There are many ways to relax and unwind after a hard day of study or work that's dragged on and on, and some are more beneficial to relaxation than others. Once you've called it a day at your computer or desk, you could opt for one of several activities, such as chilling out on the sofa with some tunes playing softly in the background. You may drift off into pleasant daydreams and easily lose track of time, helping your mind forget the hard work and challenges of the day.

If you have time on your hands, you might also partake in some gentle exercise, such as yoga, stretching or swimming. Focussing on your body may empty your mind of worrying thoughts, readying you for a peaceful night's sleep.

Have you been especially busy during the day, the latter style of activity can be of particular benefit. While it's true that some people feel more energised after doing any form exercise, however low-impact, ensure that it is done at least a couple of hours before settling down to sleep, so your heartbeat doesn't go sky-high. Not only will your body then be relaxed, but it will be fitter. This also reaps psychological rewards.

In conclusion, there is no one way of relaxing after a busy or stressful day of studying or working, but those activities which benefit both mind and body may be the best way to leave your troubles behind for the evening.

EXAM TIP

Read the whole task first. Think about how to answer the question, then choose the two bullet points you can answer most fully. You may use the ideas in the quotes, but should put them into your own words.

EXAM TASK — WRITING PART 1

You have had a discussion in class about making the best use of free time.

You have made the notes below:

> How should we spend our free time?
> - engaging in new experiences
> - relaxing alone
> - being with others

> Some opinions expressed in the discussion:
>
> 'We've got to fit in as many experiences as we can. We only live once!'
>
> 'Doing nothing for a while helps us switch off.'
>
> 'Spending quality time with family and friends is more important than anything else.'

Write an essay discussing **two** of the ways in your notes of spending free time. You should **explain which you think is a more effective way for people to spend their free time, giving reasons** to support of your answer.

You may, if you wish, make use of the opinions expressed in the discussion, but you should use your own words as far as possible.

4 Write your answer to the exam task in 220–260 words in an appropriate style.

SELF-EVALUATION

Check your writing:

Content: Have you addressed all three points and made use of the notes you made? ☹ ☺ 😐 ☺

Communication: Have you fully explained your ideas and opinions and given reasons for your answers? ☹ ☺ 😐 ☺

Organisation: Is your essay organised appropriately, and have you made use of a variety of cohesive devices? ☹ ☺ 😐 ☺

Language: Have you used a range of vocabulary and grammatical structures accurately? ☹ ☺ 😐 ☺

HAVING AN OPEN AND RESPECTFUL DISCUSSION

Do you prefer having a discussion with one person or in a group? Why?
Which topics do you enjoy discussing the most? Which topics don't you like to discuss? Why?

My group members are: _____
_____

The topic we have chosen is: _____
_____

1 EXPRESSING MY OPINION WITH SUPPORTING REASONS

I agree/disagree with the statement because:
- _____
- _____
- _____
- _____

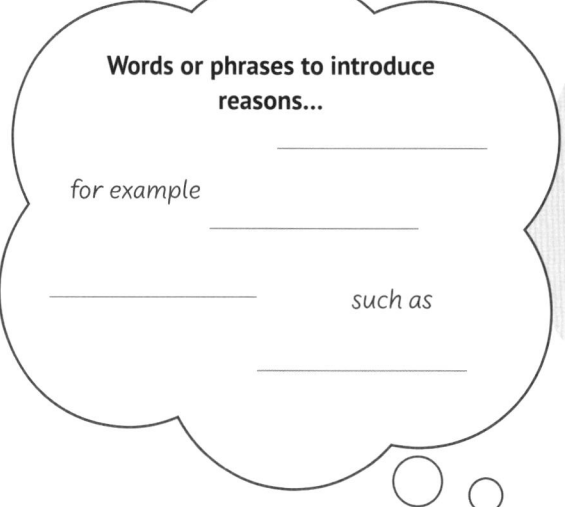

Words or phrases to introduce reasons...

_____

for example _____

_____ such as

_____

2 RESPECTING THE FEELINGS AND VIEWS OF OTHERS

How can you respect the feelings and views of others? Write down ideas from the video, then add your own ideas.

Do	Don't
	interrupt

46 | UNIT 5 TIME OUT

3 USING A WIDE RANGE OF LINGUISTIC DEVICES

ORACY 3

Take one of your arguments and improve it using inversion.

| I don't feel relaxed until I switch my phone off. Only once I switch my phone off do I feel relaxed. |

If you can, record your discussion and watch it back. Does anything you do surprise you?

Reflections on the discussion

Things that went well:
_____
_____

Things that could be improved:
_____
_____

How you respected the opinions and ideas of others:
_____
_____

Things you did well as a group:
_____
_____

Things you could improve as a group:
_____
_____

Choose another topic from the options OR make a list of other topics you would like to discuss.

Discussion topics …
Have another discussion.
Try to improve on the things you noted above.

SELF-EVALUATION

I can …
- express my opinions with supporting reasons.
- respect the feelings and views of others.
- use a wide range of linguistic devices.
- listen properly to others.

UNIT 5 TIME OUT | 47

UNIT 6 WHAT'S IN A WORD?

VOCABULARY

MULTI-WORD VERBS: COMMUNICATION

1 Match the sentence halves.

1 I told Marisa not to tell anyone about my birthday, but she just blurted
2 My younger sister is always getting in trouble for answering
3 I know you're shy, but you can come
4 I wish you had talked me
5 I think it's really important to speak
6 I didn't understand what Mia was going
7 My boss doesn't want to let me
8 I love music, so I'm glad you talked me
9 Raul is so annoying. He always talks
10 He was really trying to get

a out of getting that spicy curry last night!
b into going to that jazz concert.
c my parents back.
d across to everyone how important it is to follow the rules.
e on about at lunchtime today.
f it out in front of the whole class.
g over everyone and never listens.
h out against injustice when you see it.
i in on what the new project is yet.
j across as rude if you don't talk to people.

2 Complete the questions with the correct form of the multi-word verbs in Exercise 1. Then write your answers to the questions.

1 What would happen if you _____ your teacher _____?
2 What is an issue that it's important to _____ about?
3 How do you feel if someone _____ you when you are speaking?
4 Has anyone ever _____ you _____ doing something you didn't really want to do?

READING

EXAM TIP

For each question, one answer choice will match an idea from the text, but it may use different wording than the original.

EXAM TASK — READING AND USE OF ENGLISH PART 5

1 You are going to read an article about language and identity. For questions 1–6, choose the answer (A, B, C or D) which you think fits best according to the text.

1 What point is exemplified by the reference to colour in the first paragraph?
   A Language is dictated by our lifestyles.
   B The language we speak influences our world view.
   C There may not be a term for a particular concept in all languages.
   D Some languages cannot describe colours.

2 What is the writer doing in the second paragraph?
   A outlining the popularity of certain languages
   B discussing the way in which common languages are created
   C explaining how language can aid cross-cultural communication
   D describing why same-language speakers understand each other well

3 The writer refers to Mei to highlight
   A the influence that the languages a person speaks have on each other.
   B the way the structure of a language forces its speakers to interact.
   C the impact using a language might have on an individual's perception of self.
   D the differences in behaviour between different language groups.

4 A sociolinguist might be interested in skateboarders because they
   A use language designed to exclude non-skaters.
   B exemplify how language is central to group identity.
   C make great efforts to fit in to a group.
   D enjoy promoting their individual identity.

5 The examples of different language communities mentioned in the fifth paragraph demonstrate
   A how adaptable we are when it comes to using different varieties of language.
   B how little control we have over our use of language in different situations.
   C how individuals seek to distinguish themselves from others through language use.
   D how other people react to the way in which we speak in different situations.

6 The final paragraph conveys sadness about
   A the decline of activity-specific languages.
   B the pace at which languages are dying out.
   C the far-reaching effects of language loss.
   D the future of minority languages.

Language and identity

Language is a means by which we communicate with others: family, friends, colleagues and acquaintances. But it is also much more than that. It is culture. It is identity. Those who speak the same first language understand each other on a deeper level, one that is more than just the definitions of the individual words. And each language explains the world in a different way. In Japanese, green and blue are described with the umbrella term *ao*, while English distinguishes between the two linguistically. The fact that English expresses a difference between green and blue and Japanese does not is an example of how world views may vary between cultures. It doesn't mean that Japanese and English speakers see the colours differently, just that the cultural significance of them is different. Of course, ways of viewing concepts doesn't just stop at colour.

Language is culture, which is why speakers of the same first language share a profound knowledge of the way their fellow first-language speakers work: their behaviour, practices, norms, beliefs and values. Even when people converse in a *lingua franca* (a language used for communication purposes all parties involved in a conversation speak), there is a mutual accord that goes beyond the words. First-language speakers have a shared history and identity, and a common language strengthens that identity. If a person's desire is to assimilate fully into another culture, having knowledge of its language is essential. The more language you acquire, the more likely it is that you will have a greater grasp of the people who speak it as a first language.

Speaking a second language can have an interesting effect on the speaker, many of whom report a sense of having a different identity in their second language from that of their first. The greater the difference in cultures, the greater this difference feels. Take Mei, a Chinese student, studying in the UK. 'When I speak in English, because I feel it reflects the culture, I feel empowered, emboldened. I speak in a more direct way, and behave more assertively than when I speak Chinese. I have a sense of individualism. Chinese culture, the way I see it, is more about the harmony of the whole, so I'm less self-focussed when I speak in Chinese. It's like I'm two different people depending on the language I'm using. Of course, this is a purely personal experience that I find truly fascinating to observe in myself.'

A branch of linguistics called sociolinguistics focuses on language use across different social groups and contexts, and helps us understand how language shapes individual and group identities. Sociolinguists are concerned with how the language we choose to use helps us express who we are in different contexts. Consider skateboarders, a group that has a very clear identity. There's the visual representation, which includes clothing, logos and graphics, but there is a skateboarding language, too. This encompasses the names of the tricks (*jumps* and *manoeuvres*) and skatepark or street features used in skateboarding. To truly become part of the community and communicate with others in it, one has to acquire the language, which in turn helps one understand its culture and history.

Most of us belong to different communities (hobbies, work, friendship groups) and communicate with ease within them. We use the expected terminology or accent to express our affiliations with our social groups. The way we interact with one group may differ quite radically from the way we speak in another situation. In the office, we adopt the lingo of the tasks and company culture; at the gym, we match the informal chat; at home, we use the common language of the household. Every human who uses speech to communicate has their own unique *idiolect*, distinctive speech made up of factors that encompass all our language varieties. We may also make decisions to opt in or out of a group through our use of language. It can also act as a marker of social status and even exclusion – desired or otherwise – from a community.

When a language is lost, its culture sometimes regrettably goes along with it. Every so often, a language drops out of use and is considered extinct once the last speaker passes away. This happens not only to national languages, but to the languages of social groups too, a hobby, say, that no one does any more. This natural phenomenont has various causes, such as globalisation, mass migration, or technological development. Each group has its own traditions and customs as well as language, and once the people who speak the language have gone, we unfortunately lose a part of the world, too. But new languages and new varieties of language pop up, too, albeit it at a slower rate, and we should be grateful at least for this.

GRAMMAR

IMPERSONAL REPORTING STRUCTURES

1 Find and correct five errors in the text.

> LearnGlobe is to be believed to be the first fully AI-integrated online virtual reality classroom for language learning. It have also been said by our learners that it is the most enjoyable way to learn a new language.
>
> Learners are believed to spending more time on learning languages due to the fun and dynamic personalised classes. Currently there are ten languages available to learn, but it is expected to be more languages available soon. The company is estimate to be investing more than $1 million in expanding its research into AI in language learning.

2 Complete the sentences with an impersonal reporting structure. Use the words in brackets.

1. There _____ (estimate / be) over 5,000 new English words created each year.
2. About 1,000 _____ (report / add) to the English dictionary each year.
3. Young people _____ (thought / create) the most new words.
4. _____ (said) that the growth of technology has helped create many new words in recent times.

3 Rewrite the sentences with an impersonal reporting structure, using the word given.

1. There is an estimated 1.5 billion language learners worldwide. **BEEN**
   It _____.
2. Experts believe it is easier to learn a new language as a child. **BELIEVED**
   It _____.
3. Researchers say that studying for one hour a day speeds up learning a language. **HAS**
   It _____.
4. Some people believe that listening to music is a good way to learn a language. **BE**
   Listening to music _____.
5. People who are bilingual earn about 5–20% more than monolingual people. **SAID**
   It has _____.

PREFERENCES, WISHES AND REGRETS

4 Read the sentences and choose the correct meaning.

1. If only I hadn't dropped my phone in the toilet!
2. I'd rather talk to people in real life than on a video call.
3. I wish I didn't waste so much time online.
4. I hope I can find my missing headphones.
5. I wish you wouldn't have the TV so loud.
6. If only I didn't need to work tonight.

a   a preference
b   a regret about the past
c   a complaint
d   a possible or likely wish
e   a wish about the future
f   a wish about the present

5 Complete the conversation with the correct form of the verbs in brackets.

6 Complete the sentences with your own ideas.

← **Sarah**
  Online

Sarah: Mum! I wish you ¹_____ (not message) me in the mornings – I'm too busy to chat.

Mum: Sorry, I'd rather ²_____ (call) you, but I have a problem and it's urgent.

Sarah: What's the matter? I hope you ³_____ (not lose) your keys again!

Mum: No, my computer has crashed. I wish I ⁴_____ (not do) that update last night! If only I ⁵_____ (leave) it alone – now it doesn't work at all.

Sarah: I'm not sure how I can help with that. I'm not the best with computers. I should ⁶_____ (study) computing at school instead of art. It would have been more useful!

Mum: I just wanted the number of your friend who fixes computers. Is it Jerry? I wish I still ⁷_____ (have) his number from the last time he helped me.

Sarah: Oh, OK. I'll send it now. I hope he ⁸_____ (be able to fix) it.

Mum: I'll call him now and tell you what he says.

Sarah: I'd sooner you ⁹_____ (not call) until I finish work. Let's do it then.

50 | UNIT 6 WHAT'S IN A WORD?

1 I shouldn't have _____.
2 I'd sooner people didn't _____.
3 I wish I had _____.
4 If only _____.
5 I hope that _____.
6 I'd rather people didn't _____.
7 I hope I will _____.
8 I hope that we don't _____.

7 >>> **STRETCH!** Complete the paragraph with one word in each gap.

I started losing my sight at the age of ten, which was around the same time I started to really love books and reading. At first, I'd ¹_____ read audiobooks than learn Braille, but now I wish I ²_____ learned Braille earlier.
Braille is a system of reading and writing based around a series of raised dots. ³_____ has been said that a good Braille reader can read up to 125 words a minute. I ⁴_____ one day I can read that quickly! Braille readers ⁵_____ believed to be able to learn more quickly the younger they start learning. Although there are around 44 million blind people worldwide, there are estimated to ⁶_____ only around six million of them that use Braille. If ⁷_____ Braille was more widely available, more people would probably learn. It is reported ⁸_____ less than 1% of books are available in Braille.

VOCABULARY

BODY LANGUAGE IDIOMS AND VERBS

1 Choose the correct answers.

1 Those exam questions were so difficult! They really had me *scratching my head / biting my tongue*.
2 Will you please sit still and stop *flinching / fidgeting*!
3 Ow! Did you need to *nudge / scowl* me so hard?
4 I can't bear programmes about hospitals. The sight of blood really makes me *shrug / squirm*.
5 I can't believe that Alan got the promotion. That will certainly *raise a few eyebrows / roll some eyes*.
6 My new cat is so nervous that she *flinches / nudges* whenever someone strokes her.
7 Lara *fidgeted / shrugged her shoulders* when I asked her what she wanted to do today, so I guess we'll have to decide.
8 My manager *scowled / flinched* at me when I came in late again.
9 Her joke was so stupid that I *scratched my head / rolled my eyes*.
10 Diego's poem was really bad, but I didn't say anything. I managed to *bite my tongue / raise my eyebrows*.

2 **Critical Thinking and Decision Making**
Which of the things in Exercise 1 might you do in these situations?

1 A toddler keeps asking you the same question again and again.
_____
2 Someone kicks a football at your head.
_____
3 Your best friend shaves all their hair off.
_____
4 Your teacher asks you a really difficult question in class.
_____

LISTENING

1 Complete the definitions with the words and phrases in the box.

> bilingual   an endangered language
> a global language   a language revival
> linguistics   a native speaker

1 _____ is a person who speaks a language as their first language
2 _____ means using or able to speak two languages
3 _____ is the scientific study of languages
4 _____ is an attempt to stop a language falling out of use, or to bring back an extinct language
5 _____ is a language that is spoken by many people around the world for communication purposes
6 _____ is a language that is under threat of dying out

2 Match the adjectives in the box to the comments.

> complacent   frustrated
> hopeful   regretful   sceptical

1 'A language can be revived if adequate efforts are made to save it.' _____
2 'Why I can't get my words out when I try to speak French is completely beyond me – I understand it perfectly!' _____
3 'Some linguists say that language is innate – how they can be so sure, I don't know.' _____
4 'I'm not going to polish up on my Portuguese before heading to Brazil. It'll be just fine.' _____
5 'If only I'd tried harder in language classes at school, I'd understand what everyone here was saying to me.' _____

EXAM TIP

Remember that the words in the questions and options may be rephrased in the recording, so listen carefully for meaning.

3 Look at question 2 of the exam task. You will not hear the words *regretful*, *pleased* or *sceptical*, or synonyms for them in the recording. How else might these feelings be expressed?

EXAM TASK   LISTENING PART 1

4 🔊 6.1 You will hear three different extracts. For questions 1–6, choose the answer (A, B or C) which fits best according to what you hear. There are two questions for each extract.

Extract One

You hear two students who are studying linguistics talking about endangered languages.

1 What is the woman's opinion about saving endangered languages?
   A It is probably a waste of time.
   B It is very difficult to implement.
   C It is impossible by a certain stage.
2 How does the man feel about efforts to revive the Welsh language?
   A regretful that so many people had stopped using it beforehand
   B pleased that Welsh appears to have a safer future than it once had
   C sceptical that the revival of other languages will be as successful

Extract Two

You hear part of a podcast about English as a global language.

3 What does the woman say about English as an international language?
   A Usage of one variety of English has overtaken other varieties.
   B The number of people who speak English is continually growing.
   C Non-native English speakers can be equally as proficient in the language.
4 What is the woman's attitude towards native speakers of English?
   A They are complacent about their knowledge of it.
   B They have no right to call it theirs in the current day.
   C They make little effort to learn other varieties of English.

Extract Three

You hear two bilingual friends talking about their language use.

5 They both think that it is important that their children
   A grow up using both languages equally.
   B have a working knowledge of the minority language.
   C make more effort to use the language of where they live.
6 The man feels that being bilingual
   A offers him no real practical advantage.
   B will probably be more useful in his future than it is now.
   C has sometimes caused unnecessary problems for him.

WRITING

A REVIEW

1. Do you use any language apps or websites to improve your language skills? What's good/not so good about the ones you use? What would you write in a review about your favourite one?

2. Read the writing task below. What language-learning activities does it mention? Which other language learning activities are there? Make notes to answer the questions.

> You see the following announcement on a language-learning website.
>
> **Reviews wanted!**
>
> Send us a review of a language-learning activity, such as a class or conversation with a fluent speaker, that you've taken part in recently.
>
> How helpful was the activity for you personally? What would have made it better? Do you think it's as useful to talk to other students of the language you're learning as it is to someone who speaks it as a first language? Why? / Why not?

EXAM TIP

Consider the purpose of the review and the target reader (who your review is for) and choose an appropriate register (informal, neutral or formal). This will help you use the right kind of language in your answer.

3. Rewrite the sentences from a model review using impersonal reporting structures.

   1. People say learning a language is challenging for even the most talented of us. (It)
   2. Researchers claim it is easier to learn a third language than a second. (A third language)
   3. People believe talking with a native speaker is the best way to improve language skills. (Talking with a native speaker)
   4. Teachers say improving your pronunciation is vital to speaking another language well. (It)

4. Read the exam task. Think about a language learning website you use to improve your skills and make notes to answer the questions.

EXAM TASK — WRITING PART 2

You see the following announcement on a language-learning website.

> **Reviews wanted**
>
> Send us a review of a website you have used to improve your knowledge of a second language.
>
> How useful was the website for what you needed? How would you improve it? Do you think that using websites can ever be as good for learning languages as talking to proficient user of a language? Why? / Why not?

Write your **review**.

5. Write your answer to the task in 220–260 words in an appropriate style.

6. **Communication** For many jobs, being bilingual or speaking a second language can be a real advantage. What professions can you think of where this is the case? How could speaking more than one language help you in your career?

SELF-EVALUATION

Check your writing:

Content: Have you answered the questions fully and given reasons for your answers? ☹ 😕 😐 🙂

Communication: Have you communicated your ideas effectively? ☹ 😕 😐 🙂

Organisation: Is your review well-organised and coherent? ☹ 😕 😐 🙂

Language: Have you used a range of vocabulary and grammatical structures accurately? ☹ 😕 😐 🙂

KEEPING LANGUAGES ALIVE

1 GETTING STARTED

extinct (adj) /ɪkˈstɪŋkt/ not existing any more

indigenous (adj) /ɪnˈdɪdʒɪnəs/ relating to the first people to live in an area

Match the indigenous people to the places (key at bottom of page).

1 Maori   a Bolivia (and other South American countries)
2 Aymara   b Thailand, Vietnam, Laos
3 Hmong   c New Zealand

Who are the indigenous people of your area?
_____

What languages are indigenous to where you live?
_____

2 THINK

Why are indigenous languages disappearing?

How can we stop this?

Why does it matter?

 TIP Don't worry too much about being accurate when you are thinking of ideas. Sometimes you might just want to write a word you think of (in English or your own language), draw a picture, circle something or underline a word.

3 EXPLORE

My group is: _____

	Name of language	Where from?	Why is it threatened?	Example words
1				
2				
3				

TIP Think about how best to work together. Do you each want to research one language? How will you share your ideas?

Key: 1 c   2 a   3 b

54 | UNIT 6 WHAT'S IN A WORD?

4 DEVELOP

EXPLORING SUSTAINABILITY 3

Choose the two languages you find most interesting. Make notes about why you find them interesting.

Language 1: _____	Language 2: _____

We are going to create a *poster / digital presentation* because _____
_____

To do this we need _____
_____

I am going to be responsible for _____
_____

TIP Think about which digital tools you can use to present your ideas. You need to make sure your posters or presentations are clear and visually attractive.

5 PRESENT

Use the checklist to check your presentation:
- Is it clear which language you are presenting? ☐
- Do you include information about where it is from, who speaks it and why it is threatened? ☐
- Do you have examples of words and phrases in your presentation? ☐
- Do you talk about your personal response (why you think it is interesting)? ☐
- Is your presentation clear and visually attractive? ☐
- Have you checked your presentation for mistakes (grammar, spelling, etc.)? ☐

TIP Posters or presentations shouldn't contain large amounts of text. Use bullet points, diagrams, maps, pictures, etc. to make them easier to read and visually more interesting.

SELF-EVALUATION

I can ...
- identify and understand problems. ○
- understand the bigger picture in relation to global issues. ○
- plan an exhibition and create a wall display or digital presentation. ○

UNIT 6 WHAT'S IN A WORD?

REVIEW 2 UNITS 4–6

GRAMMAR 4

1 Complete the sentences with the correct comparative or superlative form of the adjectives in the box.

> bad (x2)   close   cool   easy
> far   good   happy   strange

1 Gregor always eats _____ food. Yesterday he had an egg and jam sandwich!
2 My little brother goes into school much _____ now that he has made some new friends.
3 I don't see Lara so often now she has moved _____ away.
4 I thought I'd done _____ in the test, but actually, I did even _____ than I thought!
5 Movie club is as _____ a club as any to meet people at.
6 Even though we don't go to the same school now, I'm still a great deal _____ to Eve than my other friends.
7 I think we're by far _____ people in our whole school!
8 It isn't as _____ to make new friends as I thought it would be.

2 Choose the correct answers to complete the text.

> As I've got older, I've realised I've got ¹ *significant / significantly* fewer friends than I used to. This might be because I don't make ² *anywhere / nowhere* near the effort I used to to meet new people. Don't get me wrong, I'm happy with the friends I have, and ³ *the fewer / the fewest* friends you have, ⁴ *the most / the more* time you can spend with them! But I wonder why, ⁵ *when / the* older you get, ⁶ *then / the* less effort you make to socialise. Is it because you become ⁷ *more and more / the most* selective about who you want to hang out with? I feel like I have ⁸ *anywhere / nowhere* near as much tolerance towards people I don't have much in common with. But is this a bad thing, because my view of the world is getting ⁹ *less and less narrow / narrower and narrower*? So, should I try to do at least ¹⁰ *slightly / considerably* more to meet new people?

VOCABULARY 4

1 Match the questions with the phrases in the box.

> bear a grudge   drift apart   enjoy your own company
> go back a long way   have ups and downs
> hit it off with someone   a shoulder to cry on
> rub you up the wrong way   strike up a friendship
> talk about someone behind their back

How would you describe …

1 someone you have known since you were five?
2 someone you haven't forgiven for something they said about you?
3 someone you used to be close to, but aren't anymore?
4 someone who is good to talk to when you have a problem?
5 someone you got along with as soon as you met them?
6 saying things about someone without them knowing?
7 someone you just can't get on with?
8 someone you just started being friends with?
9 someone you both get on with and fall out with?
10 someone who likes being alone?

2 Correct the sentences with incorrect adjectives. Two of the sentences are correct.

1 I felt really **idealistic** in my new work uniform. I don't think it suits me at all.
2 She told me it was the best essay she had ever read, but I'm not sure she was being **reserved.**
3 There's no point getting **laid-back** about the match – just do your best.
4 My dad is very **self-conscious** about politicians so he never bothers to vote.
5 I'm never sure if your brother is being serious or **sarcastic** when he says my cakes are delicious.
6 My sister is very **cynical** about time keeping, which is why she is always late!
7 Your cousin seems nice, but I haven't spoken to her much. She's always so quiet and **self-assured**.
8 I wish I was as **outgoing** as my friend Hannah. She makes friends everywhere she goes!

3 Which of the adjectives in Exercise 2 do you think are good qualities in a friend? Which are bad qualities?

GRAMMAR 5

1 Use the prompts to complete the sentences. Make any changes necessary.

1. he / finish dinner / be hungry again
   No sooner _____.
2. be earlier / I / start watching a film
   Had _____.
3. get home yesterday / I / relax
   Only once _____
4. be / give a choice, / I / start work at 10 am
   Were I _____.
5. drinking coffee in the evening / keep you awake, / make you stressed
   Not only _____.
6. she / leave the house / see the bus leave
   Hardly had _____.

2 Complete the text with the correct form of the phrasal verbs in the box. Add a pronoun if necessary.

> bring forward   come up   get up   head off
> hold up   jump on   let down   pick up
> rush around   whip up

My friend Milo is late to everything! I often ¹_____ to take him to college, but he's never ready when I get to his house. He's always ²_____ late, or he's ³_____ looking for something, or he needs to ⁴_____ some lunch. But then it ⁵_____ and I'm late too! Maybe next time I should ⁶_____ without him and he can ⁷_____ a bus instead? I'd feel bad ⁸_____ though. Or perhaps I should ⁹_____ the time I say I'll be there so he's earlier? I do need to ¹⁰_____ with a solution though, as it's making me stressed!

3 Complete the text with one word in each gap.

This morning, no sooner had I woken up, ¹_____ I realised my bed was surrounded by water! I ²_____ up carefully and went down to the lounge. Here I realised that not only had my bedroom been flooded, ³_____ the whole of my house. No ⁴_____ had I seen this, than I heard my brother crying. I tried to calm him ⁵_____ while I worked out what to do. Then my neighbour arrived and rang ⁶_____ her friend who works for the water company. Had she not turned up, I don't know what I ⁷_____ have done!

VOCABULARY 5

1 Complete the paragraphs with the correct form of the phrases in the box.

> behind the times   call it a day   for good
> for the time being   have time on your hands
> in a flash   in the nick of time   kill time
> lose track of time   move with the times
> on the spur of the moment
> once in a blue moon

My dad tries to ¹_____, but he is actually so ²_____ it's embarrassing. For example, ³_____ he tries to make a video call, but he always puts his hand over the camera!

My train was delayed for an hour today so I decided to ⁴_____ by going to the park to read my book. The problem was that I ⁵_____ and nearly missed the train! I had to run to the station and just jumped on ⁶_____.

Jenny and Mickey have been arguing a lot lately, so they decided to ⁷_____ and break up. The problem is, Jenny thinks they are over ⁸_____, but Michael thinks it's just ⁹_____ and that they'll get back together.

The other day I ¹⁰_____ so, ¹¹_____, I decided to watch some fun videos online, and before I knew it, an hour had passed ¹²_____!

2 Complete the email with the correct form of the multi-word verbs in the box.

> catch up on   bring forward   drag on   fit in
> fly by   hold up   lag behind   rush around

Dear Students,
Due to the ¹_____ on our practical sessions because of the art studio fire, there will be sessions to ²_____ the missed work. This is so you don't start to ³_____ when working on your portfolios, then have to ⁴_____ to finish them off in June. This term is very busy and will ⁵_____.
Because of this, I have ⁶_____ our theory session to 9 am next week. This will allow us to ⁷_____ a practical session afterwards.
Also, I'm sorry that the problem accessing Studio 1 is still ⁸_____. It should be resolved next week.
Regards,
Dr. Ramie

REVIEW 2 | 57

REVIEW 2 UNITS 4–6

GRAMMAR 6

1 Use the verbs given to rewrite the direct speech using an impersonal reporting structure.

1 'Children who are bilingual will often start speaking later.' (expect)
2 'You should watch TV or listen to podcasts in the language you are learning.' (recommend)
3 'William Shakespeare invented more than 1,700 new words.' (said)
4 'Chinese Mandarin is the most difficult language to learn.' (consider)

2 Complete the text with the words and phrases in the box.

> hadn't   hope   if only   sooner
> will   wish   would   would rather

I'm having a great time in Delhi. I'm even speaking some Hindi! I ¹_____ I had continued speaking it to my parents as I got older. If only I ²_____ thought it was embarrassing to speak another language. Here, a couple of my aunts ³_____ speak to me in Hindi, so I use my phone to translate. I ⁴_____ by the time I leave I'll be able to speak a bit better. ⁵_____ we could study Hindi at school. I'd ⁶_____ learn that than French! I ⁷_____ practise with my dad when I get home so I don't forget everything – I ⁸_____ love to be able to chat fluently one day.

SELF-ASSESSMENT!

3 Look back at your work in Units 4–6.

- ☐ comparatives and superlatives
- ☐ inversion and fronting
- ☐ multi-word verbs
- ☐ impersonal reporting structures
- ☐ preferences, wishes and regrets

1 Tick ✓ the area of grammar that you feel most confident about.
2 Circle the area of grammar that you need to work on more.
3 Underline the area of grammar that you think you will use most in future.

VOCABULARY 6

1 Complete the questions with the correct prepositions. Then answer the questions for you.

1 What do you think is worse, to answer a teacher _____ or to talk _____ them? Why?
2 What is something you could never be talked _____ doing?
3 What issue are people in your country currently speaking _____ about?
4 How would you feel if someone blurted _____ a secret about you?

2 Replace the phrases in bold with the correct form of the verbs and idioms in the box.

> bite your tongue   fidget   nudge   raise
> (a few) eyebrows   roll your eyes   scowl
> scratch your head   squirm

1 My friend wasn't listening when she was asked a question so I give her a **push with my elbow**.
2 I don't think the lady in that shop likes me – she always **looks annoyed** when I go in there.
3 My grandad tells terrible jokes that make me **feel embarrassed**.
4 Since my brother turned into a teenager he **obviously disagrees** with whatever we say.
5 My aunt constantly tells me studying art is a waste of time, but I just **stay quiet**.
6 Will you please **stop moving around** while I try to paint your nails!
7 I'm really **thinking hard** about what I'm going to get for my dad's birthday.
8 Suzi's new hairstyle certainly **made a few people look surprised**!

SELF-ASSESSMENT!

3 Look back at your work in Units 4–6.

- ☐ friendship
- ☐ personality traits
- ☐ expressions about time
- ☐ multi-word verbs: time and communication
- ☐ body language idioms and verbs

1 Tick ✓ the vocabulary group that you enjoyed learning about the most.
2 Circle the vocabulary group that you need to work on more.
3 Underline the vocabulary group that you think you will use most in future.

VOCABULARY REFERENCE 4-6

UNIT 4

bear a grudge feel long-lasting dislike towards someone for something bad they said or did to you
drift apart become less friendly with someone over time
enjoy your own company be happy to be alone
go back a long way know someone for a long time
ups and downs a mixture of good and bad experiences
hit it off get on well immediately
a shoulder to cry on someone who listens sympathetically to your problems
rub you up the wrong way irritate you
strike up a friendship start a friendship
talk about someone behind their back say bad things about a person in their absence
cynical think people are only interested in themselves
idealistic see the good in people and situations
laid-back very relaxed
outgoing confident and friendly
reserved dislike talking about your feelings
sarcastic say the opposite of what you mean, normally to criticise something or someone
self-assured confident in your own abilities
self-conscious worried what people think of you
sincere honest
uptight often worried and find it difficult to relax

UNIT 5

behind the times not fashionable or modern
call it a day stop doing something, especially working
for good forever
for the time being for the present moment
have time on your hands have nothing to do
in a flash immediately or very quickly
in the nick of time just before it is too late
kill time do something while you are waiting for something else to happen
lose track of time fail to notice time passing
move with the times become more modern
on the spur of the moment on impulse
once in a blue moon very rarely
catch up on do something that you have not been able to do recently
bring forward make the date or time of an event earlier

drag on go or pass very slowly
fit in find time to deal with someone or something
fly by go or pass very quickly
hold up delay
lag behind not keep the same pace as others
rush around try to do many things quickly

UNIT 6

answer (someone) back speak rudely when answering someone in authority
blurt out say something impulsively
come across (as) behave in a way that makes people think you have a certain characteristic
get something across make someone understand something
go on about talk about something for a long time, often in an annoying way
let someone in on something tell someone a secret
speak out express your feelings openly, especially when you disagree with something
talk someone into something persuade someone to do something
talk someone out of something persuade someone not to do something
talk over discuss a problem or situation with someone
bite your tongue stop yourself from saying something
fidget make continuous, small movements, for example because you are nervous or bored
flinch make a sudden, small movement because of pain or fear
nudge push something or someone gently, especially to push someone with your elbow
raise (a few) eyebrows cause surprise or shock
roll your eyes move your eyes upwards to show you are annoyed or bored
scowl look at someone or something with a very annoyed expression
scratch your head think hard about something
shrug (your shoulders) raise and lower your shoulders to show you do not know or are not interested
squirm move from side to side in an awkward way, because of nervousness, embarrassment, or pain

DIGITAL CLASSROOM
PRACTICE EXTRA UNITS 4-6

UNIT 7 COMMUNITY SPIRIT

VOCABULARY

COMMUNITY AND BELONGING

1 Match 1–12 to a–l to make words and phrases from Unit 7. Are the words and phrases positive, negative, or neutral?

1	close-knit	a	alienation
2	connected-	b	society
3	dis-	c	community
4	face-to-face	d	environment
5	mainstream	e	sider
6	meaningful	f	isolation
7	out-	g	ness
8	peer	h	group
9	sense of	i	of belonging
10	sense	j	connection
11	social	k	interaction
12	supportive	l	connections

2 Complete the paragraph with words and phrases from Exercise 1.

> **Moving to a new area for work or study can be a real challenge.**
>
> It's especially hard if you're moving to a small or ¹_____. No one likes feeling like an ²_____.
> Of course, some places of work or study offer a ³_____ that will help you to integrate into the area. However, some people find they have a better sense of ⁴_____ among existing networks online, particularly if you feel you don't fit into ⁵_____ and can find more ⁶_____ with people online with the same interests. This can lead to a ⁷_____ with people in the offline world, though. We need to feel a ⁸_____ in our communities, not a ⁹_____. To avoid ¹⁰_____, try to find opportunities to have ¹¹_____ with people in your ¹²_____, perhaps by joining clubs or sports teams, or trying to find people with shared interests.

3 **Emotional Intelligence** Imagine there is a new person starting at school or work. How could you help create a supportive environment for them? Think about what sort of practical and emotional support they might need.

READING

1 You are going to read four texts written by people who live or have lived on remote islands. What positive or negative aspects of island life might they mention?

2 Read the texts quickly and check your ideas.

EXAM TIP

Read all the texts quickly to find out what they are about, then read text A very carefully and choose all the questions that it answers. Do the same for the other texts.

✓ EXAM TASK READING AND USE OF ENGLISH PART 8

3 You are going to read an article in which four writers talk about living on a small island. For questions 1–10, choose from the writers (A–D). The writers may be chosen more than once.

Which writer

mentions people being surprised about one aspect of where the island is situated?	1
describes an immediate feeling of belonging in a place?	2
mentions a longing to be in a particular setting?	3
conveys a sense of pride in the island's unique landscapes?	4
acknowledges that relationships can sometimes be strained?	5
refers to an assumption made by other people about what life is like on the island?	6
mentions a feeling of being limited in terms of life experiences?	7
explains the occasional need to depend on others?	8
points out that there are pros and cons associated with living in a popular place?	9
admits that one feature of the community is more beneficial than it sounds?	10

Living on a Remote Island

A Heather Anderson

I grew up on a small Scottish island, one of the most remote off the coast of Scotland. It has some of the most stunningly beautiful beaches in Britain, with startlingly white sands that are reminiscent of those found in tropical places, far removed from the typical UK coastline. Luckily for the island's inhabitants, it's tricky to reach, so they don't need to share its beauty with thousands of day-trippers. Just over a thousand people live there, which means everyone knows your business! Despite the lack of privacy that might suggest, living in a close-knit community is actually a blessing in disguise: there'll always be someone to lend a hand with a job around the home or on the land, or just generally look out for you. Of course, I recognise that now looking back, but as a young teenager, it wasn't quite so desirable to have parents potentially breathing down our necks all the time! Though to be fair to them, we were free to do pretty much as we wanted. I no longer live on the island – I had to move for work – but I maintain my sense of connectedness with it and visit whenever I get the chance. It will always be the place I call home.

B Kamilah Sari

People from the mainland often ask whether there's a feeling of social isolation living where I do, which is a tiny island in Indonesia. If other residents feel that, it's alien to me. I see only advantages living at close quarters with family and friends. It's like everyone you know is just an extension of your actual family, and we do our best to get along, whatever the situation. I believe we form meaningful connections quickly and forever, even with newcomers. I often hear visitors call the island 'paradise' and they expect a holiday vibe everywhere, which isn't the case for locals going about their daily business. Tourism's a double-edged sword. On the one hand, we benefit greatly from it; on the other, it creates a strain on resources for local people, in addition to environmental concerns. But it also means having frequent face-to-face interactions with people from many other countries, which promotes cross-cultural understanding and opportunities for education all round. That's probably what I like most about where I'm from.

C Leif Solberg

I live on a remote Norwegian archipelago. It's in the Arctic Circle and has some pretty wild and rugged terrain, which can create transportation challenges. The region has been inhabited for at least 11,000 years, which seems to take some people aback because of its location far from major cities. It's a harsh place to be during the winter months, with howling gales and a good few layers of snow. I think that's what has created a supportive environment for those who live there. Sometimes, there's little option but to hitch lifts, borrow fuel, and even food should you happen to get cut off. That doesn't mean everyone's the best of friends – nowhere on Earth can really be like that, and minor tensions arise in small communities where it's tricky to create distance. That said, it's also probably easier to make up – there's little point in harbouring resentments or bearing a grudge, given the circumstances surrounding people's existence here.

D Matias Araya

I moved to an island off the coast of Chile after years of living in a vast, sprawling city that could literally take hours to traverse – or get out of. I tended to stick to the same neighbourhood, and even though in theory there was everything I could ever want 'on my doorstep', in reality, it was just too much hassle to bother, and it actually felt more restricting than if I'd lived in a village halfway up a mountain! On the rare occasion I did leave the city to go on holiday, I'd head straight for the coast. Ultimately, the call of the ocean was strong enough to pull me there permanently. I never felt like an outsider; right from the word go, people welcomed me with open arms, eager for tales of big city life, but also through genuine warmth and interest. There's a real sense of community here, but without people poking their noses into your business; it's a real 'live and let live' kind of place.

GRAMMAR

MODAL VERBS EXTENSION

1 Complete the sentences with the correct form of a verb in the box. Add any extra words that are necessary.

> able allow ban entitle free manage
> oblige permit require suppose

Welcome to Figero, a great community where we all look out for each other. While you are staying in the holiday home, please follow these simple instructions:

1 You _____ put all the rubbish in the bins outside at the end of your stay and to leave all dirty towels in the bath.

2 You _____ having parties or playing loud music after 10 pm.

3 Guests _____ to use the garden and the barbecue.

4 If you _____ connect to the internet, try turning the modem off for ten seconds. The wi-fi password is on the fridge.

5 Unfortunately, you _____ have pets to stay in the holiday home.

6 There are basic condiments in the kitchen cupboard. You _____ use them.

7 You _____ to leave the property by 10 am on your final day.

2 Which of the sentences in Exercise 1 express:

A prohibition? _____
B obligation? _____
C permission/right? _____
D ability? _____

3 Find and correct six errors in the text.

At Mill Farm community gardens, everyone are able to help grow their own fruit and vegetables. Volunteers are suppose to commit to working in the gardens for at least half a day every week, but if you can managed to help more, then that is very much appreciated! You are free choosing the type of task you help with; for example, planting, weeding, preparing vegetable bags or working on the market stall. However, you are required commit to the same job for a month before changing roles. The exception to this is new volunteers, who allow to try out a number of different roles before deciding which one they prefer.

4 Answer the questions with modal verbs from Exercise 1. If you were in charge of your town, what is one thing:

1 you would prohibit?
   _____

2 you would oblige people to do?
   _____

3 you would give permission for?
   _____

4 everyone would be able to do?
   _____

COMPLEX PREPOSITIONS

5 Match the words in the columns to make complex prepositions.

> by (x2)
> for
> in (x5)
> on (x2)
> with

> account aid
> behalf   charge
> keeping line
> means   regard
> return
> the sake way

> for
> of (x7)
> to
> with (x2)

6 Complete the letter with the correct complex prepositions in Exercise 5.

Blogs Newsletters   Search...

Dear Residents,
I'm writing to you all ¹_____ some exciting events that are coming up.

Firstly, we have a community barbecue and fair next Saturday in Riverbend Park. This is ²_____ the new skatepark that we are raising money to build. There will also be someone there ³_____ the skatepark design company to talk through the design. This company is working hard to make a skatepark that is ⁴_____ the local environment and would appreciate any community feedback.

Secondly, ⁵_____ new fire safety guidance that has recently been released, we are having a training day at the fire station on the 22nd October. ⁶_____ a donation to the fire station, the fire officer ⁷_____ the station will be offering a two-hour training session. Don't worry if you can't attend on the day, as there will also be training and information offered ⁸_____ an online course. Details to follow.

7 >>> STRETCH! Complete the second sentence so that it has a similar meaning to the first, using the word given.

1 Students can leave the college at lunchtime if they want to. **FREE**
  Students _____.

2 To apologise, they gave me a discount on my rent. **MEANS**
  By _____.

3 You should have helped your grandmother with her shopping. **SUPPOSED**
  You _____.

4 Due to rising costs, our meal deal is now £5.50. **ACCOUNT**
  Our meal deal _____.

5 If you don't finish your project in class, you need to finish it at home. **MANAGE**
  If you can't _____.

6 Try to keep the noise down at night so you don't annoy the neighbours. **SAKE**
  For _____.

VOCABULARY

URBANISATION

1 Choose the correct answers to complete the paragraph.

Many cities in recent years have undergone a process of urban ¹ *sprawl / renewal* in order to make them more suitable for the modern world. Urbanisation can quickly lead to ² *overcrowding / housing*, with not enough ³ *green belt / amenities* such as hospitals or schools to support the growing population. When cities have grown more quickly than the ⁴ *infrastructure / congestion* needed to support them, town planners need to work out the best way to organise water supplies, telecommunications and transport links (in order to avoid ⁵ *traffic congestion / amenities*).

Often, due to the need for more ⁶ *infrastructure / housing*, ⁷ *urban sprawl / overcrowding*, where the city expands and expands, occurs. One way to counteract this is by creating ⁸ *a green belt / urban renewal* around a city.

2 Think about the city you live in, or your nearest city. Answer the questions for you.

1 What amenities are there? Are there any amenities it needs?

2 Are there problems with overcrowding or traffic congestion? If yes, what do you think could be done to improve this?

3 Is there an issue with urban sprawl? Is there a green belt? If not, do you think this would be a good idea?

4 Is there enough housing? Does it have a good infrastructure? How could housing or infrastructure be improved?

LISTENING

1 What do you think would be difficult when moving to a new country? Make a list.

2 Match the terms for talking about people who move to a new country 1–3 to the definitions a–c.

1 immigrant
2 migrant
3 refugee

a A person who has left their country due to political reasons, war, natural disasters, etc.
b A person who travels to a different place or country, often to look for work.
c A person who has come from another country to live permanently.

3 🔊 7.1 Listen to the presentation. Which factors from your list in Exercise 1 are mentioned? Which other difficulties are mentioned?

4 🔊 7.1 Listen again. Complete the sentences with words from the presentation. Use no more than six word in each gap.

1 Most migrants to Spain come from _____.
2 'Unaccompanied minors' are people under the age of _____.
3 Football could be called _____.
4 FC Darna choose the name of their football team because it _____.
5 Young migrants are inspired by Nico Williams and Lamine Yamal because they _____.
6 Players at A.E Ramassa come from places _____.
7 Aitana Bonmatí spoke to women footballers about the difficulties they have such as coming from countries where _____.
8 Football clubs can help people become a part of _____.

5 🔊 7.1 Which phrases about community and belonging did you hear in the presentation? Listen again and make a list.

6 Answer the questions for you.

1 Do you think sport is a good way to help immigrants? Why? /Why not?
2 What other ways can you think of to help immigrants become a part of mainstream society?
3 Do you have many immigrants in your community? If so, where do they come from and why?

WRITING

A PROPOSAL

1 Which of the following might be described as fun community events?

> a day of dance   a clean-up event
> a communal picnic   a council meeting
> a food fair   a municipal concert
> a play in the park   a town festival

2 Imagine you are organising one of the events in Exercise 1. Answer the questions.

1 Where would the event be held?
2 What activities would it include?
3 How could it be made suitable for people of all ages and backgrounds?
4 What would the advantages be for those who attended it?

3 Read the exam task below. Look at the questions in Exercise 2 and make notes on ideas for the event.

> Your neighbourhood community centre would like to put on an event to help neighbours get to know each other better. Residents of your local area have been asked to submit a proposal for an event that might encourage neighbourhood friendships. You decide to write a proposal to the community centre, suggesting an event, explaining how it might encourage friendships in the neighbourhood, and saying how this will benefit local people.

64 | UNIT 7 COMMUNITY SPIRIT

4 Read the proposal. How do the writer's ideas differ from your own?

> **Back**
>
> **Introduction**
>
> I am writing to present a proposal for an event to encourage friendships amongst neighbours.
>
> **The event**
>
> In my opinion, the community centre is an ideal venue for a neighbourhood event. A 'sharing' afternoon would allow people to get to know other and encourage face-to-face interaction. People could bring along a dish to share, or teach others a skill they have. In addition, there could be a 'coffee and chat' area, or games in aid of prompting social interaction. Including a range of activities would mean that there is something for everyone of all backgrounds, genders and ages.
>
> **Encouraging friendships**
>
> Who doesn't benefit from having fun and lively conversation with others? People will be able to meet others in their local community that they may not have spent time with previously, or otherwise have been accepting of. I strongly believe that this will promote understanding and help people to make new friends with shared interests.
>
> **Benefits to local people**
>
> With regard to the benefits of such an event, young and old alike will gain from teaching each other about their lives, sharing wisdom and ideas across the generations. People's social circles will be expanded and a supportive environment will be created, something especially helpful for residents who are isolated, elderly or infirm.
>
> **Conclusion**
>
> I am of the firm view that holding a community sharing day will bring people closer together to enjoy new and meaningful connections, and similarly improve community spirit.

5 Read the proposal again. Find examples of the following:

1. complex prepositions _____
2. a rhetorical question _____
3. emotive adjectives _____
4. connectors _____
5. language of opinion _____

EXAM TIP

Read the task carefully and decide what to write for each of the points you have to answer. Remember to use an appropriate tone for the target reader and provide examples to support your main points.

6 Read the exam task below. How many points do you need to include? Make notes for each point and decide how you will organise the information into relevant sections.

✓ EXAM TASK   WRITING PART 2

> Your local council would like to hold a community event to bring people closer together in the town. Residents have been asked to submit suggestions for an event they think people from different backgrounds could enjoy together. Write a proposal to the council suggesting an event, explaining what people might enjoy about it, and saying how you think it would bring people closer together.
>
> Write your **proposal**.

7 Write your answer in 220–260 words in an appropriate style.

SELF-EVALUATION

Check your writing:

Content: Is all the content relevant to the task, and will the target reader be fully informed?   ☹ ☹ 😐 🙂

Communication: Have you used an appropriate format and clearly communicated your opinions?   ☹ ☹ 😐 🙂

Organisation: Is your proposal well-organised and coherent?   ☹ ☹ 😐 🙂

Language: Have you used a range of vocabulary and grammatical structures accurately?   ☹ ☹ 😐 🙂

MANAGING CONFLICT

My ideas and solutions:
Situation 1: Luke and Tara
Situation 2: Maya and Jamal

How do you feel about dealing with conflict? Why?

1 USING VOCABULARY TO MODERATE DEBATES

Which of these phrases do you think would help when there is a conflict and which do you think you shouldn't say? Tick the phrases you think are best.

Calm down! ☐
What do you think we could do to resolve this? ☐
What's your problem? ☐
I hear what you are saying. ☐
Chill out. ☐
I can see you are upset. ☐
Can you think of any other good phrases to use?

2 RESPECTING THE FEELINGS AND VIEWS OF OTHERS IN A DISCUSSION

Phrases for building on others ideas:	Phrases for politely disagreeing:

UNIT 7 COMMUNITY SPIRIT

3 CONTROLLING THE VOLUME OF MY VOICE

ORACY 4

How true are these statements for you? (1 = not true at all, 5 = very true)

1	When I'm in a conflict I normally shout.	1	2	3	4	5
2	When someone shouts it makes me more angry.	1	2	3	4	5
3	If there is an argument, I normally become very quiet.	1	2	3	4	5
4	I think shouting is always a bad idea in a conflict.	1	2	3	4	5
5	I only shout if someone talks over me.	1	2	3	4	5
6	People listen to people who shout more.	1	2	3	4	5

Compare your answers in pairs. Which things do you think you could improve?

My group is me, _____ and _____.
My role is Maya / Jamal / Observer.

Notes (e.g. phrases to use, points to make, things to look for).
_____
_____
_____

Reflections on the discussion

Things that went well:
_____
_____

Things that could be improved:
_____
_____

Good language used:
_____
_____

Volume of voices:
_____
_____

After the discussion:
How do you think the characters felt after the discussion? Were they both happy?
Did you manage to reach a solution? If yes, what was it? If no, why not?

SELF-EVALUATION

I can ...
- respect and build on the feelings of others in a discussion. ○
- use vocabulary and phrases effectively to moderate debates. ○
- control the volume of my voice to avoid aggravating conflict. ○
- work with others to reach a compromise or solution. ○

UNIT 7 COMMUNITY SPIRIT

UNIT 8 IT'S NOT FAIR!

VOCABULARY

PROGRESS AND ACHIEVEMENT COLLOCATIONS

1 Choose the correct answers to complete the report.

Robbie has really **¹** *risen to the challenge / broken the records* of this year and **²** *exceeded / suffered* many of his teachers' **³** *setbacks / expectations*. Despite **⁴** *overcoming an obstacle / suffering a setback* when he broke his arm in May, he continued to **⁵** *lead the way / pursue his goal* of making the school basketball team. He also **⁶** *set a target / leads the way* in the athletics club where he has **⁷** *pursued / broken* several school **⁸** *goals / records*. By **⁹** *rising to the challenge / overcoming the obstacle* of his injury, he showed great determination. We also see this in his academic work, where he is **¹⁰** *making good headway / hampering progress*, particularly in maths.

At times, however, his focus on sport can **¹¹** *exceed expectations / hamper his progress* in other areas, so we have asked him to **¹²** *make / set* himself a **¹³** *headway / target* of improving his overall grades next year.

2 ›››**STRETCH!** Complete the questions with one word in each gap. Then answer them for you.

1 What targets have you _____ yourself for the next year?
2 What (place, film, etc) exceeded your _____?
3 Do you think you are _____ headway in learning English?
4 When is a time you have suffered a _____?

EXAM TIP

As you read the text for the first time, consider what kind of word might fit in each gap, for example, an auxiliary verb, a preposition, a phrasal verb particle, a conjunction, or a determiner.

READING AND USE OF ENGLISH

1 Quickly read the text about the United Nations (UN)'s Sustainable Development Goals. Are the sentences true or false?

1 The UN's goals are challenging to achieve.
2 The vast majority of countries are reaching their educational targets.
3 Only a minority of countries are fulfilling the UN's goal of ensuring quality education.

✓ EXAM TASK — READING AND USE OF ENGLISH PART 2

2 For questions 1–8, read the text below and think of the word which best fits each gap. Use only one word in each gap. There is an example at the beginning (0).

The United Nation's Sustainable Goals

The United Nations (UN) is an organisation which aims, amongst many things, **(0)** ___to___ maintain international peace and security. Its 17 Sustainable Development Goals aim to promote a fairer world for everyone. **(1)** _____ of these is to 'Ensure inclusive and equitable quality education and promote lifelong learning opportunities for all'.

The need for **(2)** _____ a goal is because the world has been falling too far **(3)** _____ in achieving its targets. **(4)** _____ numbers of children completing primary and secondary education are rising, progress is slow and uneven. **(5)** _____ additional measures should fail to be put in place, there is a very real danger that **(6)** _____ under a decade's time, there could be as **(7)** _____ as 84 million children and young people out of school, and only one in six countries **(8)** _____ definitely manage to meet the universal secondary school completion target. It is therefore imperative that the world works harder at delivering the UN's goals.

68 | UNIT 8 IT'S NOT FAIR!

READING

1 How are criminals in your country punished for different crimes? Make a list.

2 Quickly read the article. Which country …

1 tries to educate young criminals? _____
2 uses dancing as a form of rehabilitation? _____
3 tries to recreate normal life in prison? _____
4 lets families stay together in prison? _____

RETHINKING PRISONS

In most countries, if you commit a serious crime, you can expect to go to prison. In some countries, such as Singapore, you can even go to jail for littering! However, many places around the world have been trying to overcome obstacles in their prison systems such as overcrowding, being expensive to run and the inability to stop inmates from re-offending. Therefore, some places have decided to experiment with ways to reform the prison system to see if there is a better way to deal with criminals.

Bastoy prison, situated on an island in Norway and having the lowest re-offending rate in all of Europe, is an excellent example of how prisons can be reimagined. This might be due to its focus on preparing prisoners for life after they are released. They do this by allowing them to live in a way similar to how they would live outside of prison. For a start, all the inmates live in separate houses for six people where everyone has their own room, but share a kitchen and other facilities. They are given one meal a day, but are expected to buy food and cook their other meals. In order to earn money to buy food and other items they might need, they can work on the prison's farm, in the laundry or look after the prison's grounds. They also have free time where they can study, swim or go fishing. Prisoners can apply to transfer to Bastoy when they have less than five years of their sentence left. Prisoners used to complain that guards didn't treat them as humans, but at Bastoy the guards treat prisoners with respect, and expect to be treated the same way in return.

Spain is another European country that is taking a more creative approach to imprisonment. It is believed to have the only prison in the world that has family cells which enables parents that have been convicted to live with their children (up to the age of three). The prison has an onsite playground and nursery school where the children can play and learn together. Then, when playtime is over, the children return to their family cells which have double beds, cots and colourful pictures of cartoon characters.

The country is also home to a scheme called *Diagrama* which is leading the way in its approach to young offenders. The scheme runs small, residential institutes for 14–23 year olds where the emphasis is firmly on education and life skills. Although there are security staff at the centres, most employees are teachers, psychologists or social workers who help equip young people with the skills they will need to reintegrate into mainstream society and pursue their goals.

It isn't just Europe that is trying to find new ways to approach the prison system though. A prison in the Philippines was once an online sensation for its videos of dancing inmates! It included dancing and choreography as part of its rehabilitation and exercise programme.

These approaches to prisons raise the question of its overall purpose: to punish or rehabilitate?

3 Are the statements true, false, or is the infomation not given?

1 It is common for countries to have issues with their prison system. ____
2 Bastoy prison is very successful at rehabilitating prisoners. ____
3 Many of the prisoners at Bastoy have been there for many years. ____
4 In Spain, many prisoners want their children with them. ____
5 There are no guards at Diagrama institutes. ____
6 Prisoners in the Philippines are allowed to use social media. ____

4 Read the last paragraph of the article again. What do you think the main purpose of prison is?

GRAMMAR

PASSIVE EXTENSION

1 Complete the article with the passive form of the verbs in brackets.

HOME BLOGS

Young people in Wolvestone can always ¹_____ (see) in the park or outside shops in the evenings or at the weekend, as there is not much to do in the local area. But now, they are hoping ²_____ (provide) with a permanent youth centre, thanks to local charity WYT (Wolvestone Youth Today). The old community centre recently closed and WYT want ³_____ (give) the opportunity to use it for young people. '⁴_____ (give) the building would be amazing', said WYT director Jacqui Cartwright. 'We're expecting ⁵_____ (provide) with some funding soon. We'd also appreciate ⁶_____ (fund) partly by the local government, who have invested very little in facilities for local young people. We're looking forward to ⁷_____ (give) the opportunity to present our ideas'. Activities and uses currently ⁸_____ (plan) for the centre include an indoor skatepark and an art room. Young people will ⁹_____ (ask) to suggest their ideas at a meeting next month. Meanwhile, the local council says that while giving the building to WYT is too expensive ¹⁰_____ (consider), the group will ¹¹_____ (consult) about other potential options.

2 Complete the sentences with the passive form of the verbs in the box. Use each verb only once.

consult   copy   include   inform   listen   tell

HR guidelines for complaints

1 We insist on _____ if an employee makes a complaint.
2 We appreciate _____ in on any emails about the complaint.
3 Employees must _____ to when they raise a concern.
4 Most employees find that _____ is the most important part of the process.
5 Employees need _____ of the result of their complaint.
6 We are happy _____ if you have any problems or questions.

3 **Communication** Is it considered polite to complain in your culture? Why? / Why not? Do you know who to speak to at your school or work if you have a complaint?

PASSIVE VERBS WITH TWO OBJECTS

4 Are the sentences 1–6 active (A) or passive (P)?
1 The other passengers didn't offer the elderly lady a seat. ___
2 He was promised a pay rise. ___
3 They gave everyone a bar of chocolate apart from me. ___
4 He told her the truth, but she didn't believe it. ___
5 A fine was given to him for littering. ___
6 The manager was shown a red card by the referee. ___

5 Rewrite the active sentences in Exercise 3 in the passive.

1 _____
2 _____
3 _____

PASSIVE FOR INFORMATION FLOW

6 Choose the sentence that puts the new information at the end, A or B.

1. Do you know if that criminal has been arrested?
   A Yes, he was spotted by a member of the public in a shop.
   B Yes, a member of the public spotted him in a shop.
2. I can't believe Greg has left school!
   A I know, apparently the headeacher asked him to leave!
   B I know, apparently he was asked to leave by the headteacher!
3. Did you find your phone?
   A Yes, it had been given to someone at reception.
   B Yes, someone at reception had been given it.
4. Do you know about the new anti-littering law?
   A Yes, I heard it was passed last week by the government.
   B Yes, I heard the government passed it last week.

7 Choose the correct options to help the information in the text flow better.

> Last year, Laura was the victim of an online scam. She wanted to buy tickets to a concert, but they'd all sold out. She looked on resale websites, but ¹*people were all selling tickets / the tickets were all being sold* for extremely high prices. Therefore, she was really excited when she saw a post on social media where a fan couldn't go to the concert, so ²*was selling their tickets / their tickets were being sold* for the same price that they'd paid for them. She sent a message to the seller who replied immediately. ³*The seller told Laura / Laura was told* to transfer the money and then they would email her the tickets. ⁴*The seller also sent Laura / Laura was also sent* copies of the receipts and emails showing the tickets were real. However, as soon as ⁵*Laura transferred the money / the money had been transferred*, the seller deleted their account and Laura couldn't find any way to contact them. Now Laura not only had no tickets, but ⁶*she'd also lost a lot of money / a lot of money had been lost*.

VOCABULARY

ADVERB-ADJECTIVE COLLOCATIONS

1 Complete the sentences with the collocations in the box.

> deadly serious   deeply shocking
> eternally grateful   fully aware
> overwhelmingly positive   strictly forbidden
> strongly opposed   utterly bizarre

1. It's _____ to take dogs into the nature reserve.
2. I'm _____ to you for bringing my passport to the airport!
3. The government is _____ to increasing immigration.
4. I thought he was joking about how much his car cost, but it turns out he was _____.
5. I found the newspaper article about sexism in the workplace _____.
6. The reaction to the news of a pay rise from next year has been _____.
7. As you are _____, phones mustn't be used in class.
8. I couldn't understand that book at all as the story was _____.

2 Answer the questions for you.

1. What is something that should be strictly forbidden in your school or workplace?
2. Who are you eternally grateful to? Why?
3. Are there any celebrities in your country that people have an overwhelmingly positive view of? Why do you think that is?
4. Are there any rules or laws that you are strongly opposed to? Why?
5. Are there any deeply shocking or utterly bizarre stories in the news at the moment? What are they?

LISTENING

1 What responsibilities do you have? Do you enjoy having responsibility? Why? / Why not?

2 You are going to listen to five people talking about responsibility. What might each person do in the following roles?
- rugby referee
- volunteer to help with the elderly
- school road safety person
- club secretary
- school parent-teacher association member

3 Read the instructions to each task. What do you need to listen for in Task One, A or B?

A Why each speaker took on responsibility.
B What responsibility each speaker took on.

What do you need to listen for in Task Two, A or B?

A The feeling each speaker has towards their responsibility.
B The way in which each speaker has understood themselves and others better.

4 Read the exam tasks and underline the key words.

EXAM TIP

As you listen a first time, scan each task and discard any options that are clearly not correct. This will help narrow down possible options and choose one answer per speaker.
Use the second listening to check your answers.

✓ EXAM TASK   LISTENING PART 4

5 🔊 8.1 You will hear five short extracts in which people are talking about taking on responsibility.

TASK ONE

For questions 1–5, choose from the list (A–H) what each person says was the trigger for taking on responsibility.

A a way to gain knowledge about a specific subject
B a desire to provide company to those who may lack it
C a chance for greater social contact
D a desire to improve organisation of a business
E an opportunity to acquire work experience
F a chance to stay involved in an activity
G a chance to give back to those who helped them
H a sense of purpose in life

Speaker 1 [1]
Speaker 2 [2]
Speaker 3 [3]
Speaker 4 [4]
Speaker 5 [5]

TASK TWO

For questions 6–10, choose from the list (A–H) what each person says they have learned about themselves and others.

A how patient they can be when it is required
B how respectful people are when necessary
C how confident they feel in a certain situation
D how open people are to change
E how much they enjoy a challenge
F how keen they are to make an impact
G how responsive people are to kindness
H how much wisdom they can acquire from others

Speaker 1 [6]
Speaker 2 [7]
Speaker 3 [8]
Speaker 4 [9]
Speaker 5 [10]

WRITING

AN ESSAY

1 Read the exam task. What is a buddy system? What information should the writer include in the essay?

> Your student council has held a discussion about the introduction of a buddy system, whereby an older student takes responsibility for supporting a younger one. You have made the notes below:
>
> > How might a buddy system benefit both older and younger students?
> > - taking responsibility
> > - behaviour
> > - confidence building
>
> > Some opinions expressed in the discussion:
> >
> > 'Buddies take responsibility for someone else to help teach them right from wrong.'
> >
> > 'Buddies will be able to encourage good behaviour towards others.'
> >
> > 'A buddy can help a younger person develop life skills such as confidence in themselves.'
>
> Write an essay in 220–260 words discussing **two** of the benefits of a buddy system in your notes. You should **explain which benefit is most useful for both older and younger students, giving reasons** in support of your answer.
>
> You may, if you wish, make use of the opinions expressed in the discussion, but you should use your own words as far as possible.

2 Complete the sentences from a model essay with the correct form of the passive verb *be*.

1. Providing they are happy _____ paired up with a buddy, young students will benefit from seeing good behaviour modelled.
2. Examples of good buddy behaviour include showing respect and _____ punctual.
3. In turn, the older student will _____ reminded of the value of their actions.
4. These social skills are too important _____ overlooked and should _____ developed by all students.

EXAM TIP
Remember to give examples and provide support for your points.

EXAM TASK — WRITING PART 1

> Your school has just held a discussion about school rules. You have made the notes below:
>
> > Which skills can students develop through being involved in making school rules?
> > - responsibility
> > - critical thinking
> > - respect
>
> > Some opinions expressed in the discussion:
> >
> > 'Making rules helps students become responsible by thinking about others.'
> >
> > 'Analysing rules develops transferable critical thinking skills.'
> >
> > 'We show respect by listening to others' opinions and sharing ideas.'
>
> Write an essay discussing **two** of the skills in your notes. You should **explain which skills students would benefit most from developing, giving reasons** in support of your answer.
>
> You may, if you wish, make use of the opinions expressed in the discussion, but you should use your own words as far as possible.

3 Write your answer in 220–260 words in an appropriate style.

SELF-EVALUATION

Check your writing:

Content: Have you covered all the relevant content points and explained your ideas? ☹ ☹ 😐 ☺

Communication: Is the target reader fully informed about your opinions and conclusions? ☹ ☹ 😐 ☺

Organisation: Is your essay well-organised, and does it make use of appropriate cohesive devices? ☹ ☹ 😐 ☺

Language: Have you used a range of vocabulary and grammatical structures accurately? ☹ ☹ 😐 ☺

THE WORLD JUSTICE CHALLENGE

1 GETTING STARTED

justice (n) /dʒʌsˈtɪs/ fairness in the way people are treated (opposite: injustice)

Justice in society: Who's most responsible? Why?
_____
_____

2 THINK

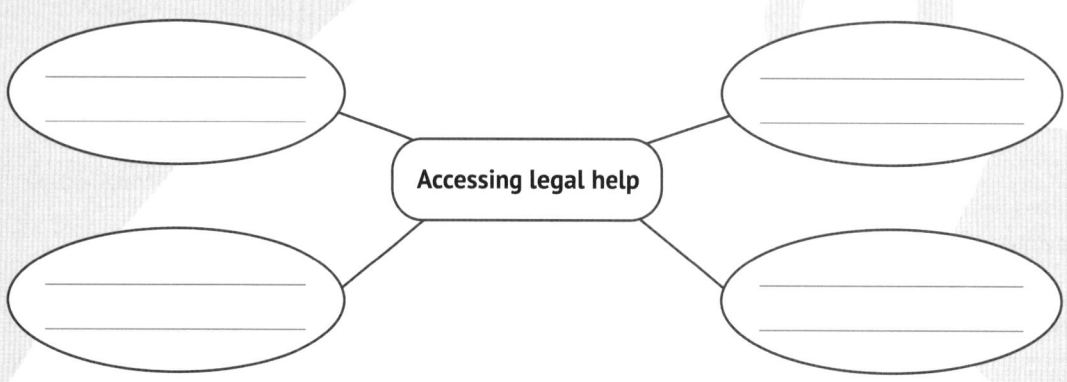

Accessing legal help

TIP Use your background knowledge when you start brainstorming a topic. Think about what happens in your country. How do people with no access to lawyers get help there?

3 EXPLORE

My group is: _____

The NGO we are going to research is: _____

Country/Area:	
Why did they start?	
What do they do?	
Who do they help?	
How do they raise funds?	
How can the public help?	

TIP Think about what digital tools would be best to share your research. Work together to agree on which one you will use and how you will divide up the research.

UNIT 8 IT'S NOT FAIR!

4 DEVELOP

EXPLORING SUSTAINABILITY 4

Highlight the information you will use in your advert in the box above.
Plan your advert below:
Format: _____
Digital tools we will use: _____
Tasks:

What?	Who?
1	
2	
3	
4	

Call to action (what do you want people to do): _____

TIP When working on a group project, think about the different skills of the group members. Maybe one person is good at design and can create the advert. Maybe one is good at writing and can write a script or text. Maybe one person is really organised and can be in charge of making sure you stick to deadlines.

5 PRESENT

TIP It's good to not only reflect upon your own work, but also other people's. Think about what they do well that you could use in your own work.

Why did you choose this NGO? Make some notes before you present your advert.
_____
_____
_____

Complete the following after you have seen all the adverts.
I think the advert with the most impact is _____
because _____.

SELF-EVALUATION

I can ...
- encourage collaborative approaches. ◯
- take accountability for my actions. ◯
- create a digital advert to attract support for a good cause. ◯
- use my existing background knowledge when approaching a task. ◯

UNIT 9 THE FAME GAME

VOCABULARY

FAME

1 Replace the words and phrases in bold in the text with the words or phrases in the box.

adulation ___	autographs ___	coverage ___
endorsements ___	glamour ___	
notoriety ___	obscurity ___	prestige ___
the scrutiny ___	show business _1_	
stardom ___	in the limelight ___	

Many young people dream of a life working in ¹**the entertainment world**. They think ²**being famous** is a life of ³**exciting and special moments**, with ⁴**the admiration and love** of fans who ask for ⁵**you to sign things** or take selfies, and many companies offering you free items in exchange for ⁶**saying how good their products are**. Of course, being famous might have some advantages, but alongside the ⁷**respect** you might get for being ⁸**well-known**, you also have to put up with ⁹**an examination** of your personal life, and perhaps negative ¹⁰**articles** in newspapers or on social media. Some people decide they would rather fade away into ¹¹**a normal life**, whereas others make a mistake and end up with the type of ¹²**negative fame** that means they can only work on reality TV shows!

READING AND USE OF ENGLISH

1 Read the text title. What might a celebrity's personal assistant do? Skim the text to find out.

2 Read the gapped sentences and look at the given words. What kind of words do you need to form?

EXAM TIP

Read the words around each gap in the text carefully to identify which part of speech you need (noun, adjective or adverb). Make sure you use a form of the given word for each gap.

EXAM TASK READING AND USE OF ENGLISH PART 3

3 For questions 1–8, read the text below. Use the word given in capitals at the end of some of the lines to form a word that fits in the gap in the same line. There is an example at the beginning (0).

Personal Assistant to a celebrity

Many people who set out on the journey to become PA to a celebrity have a (0) ___tendency___ to dream big. This often involves travelling around the world, attending (1) _____ parties and hanging out with the rich and famous. What aspiring PAs may overlook is the (2) _____ challenging schedule, the unusual chores they're tasked with and perhaps a (3) _____ personality to deal with.
What does the role actually entail? It involves the (4) _____ of 24-hour support to a high-profile individual, who may work in music, fashion, film or another related industry. PAs often find themselves working in a highly (5) _____ environment, meeting the needs of someone who is used to getting what they want when they want it.
A PA may bear responsibility for (6) _____ diary management, the organisation of international travel, and liaising with other members of the celebrity's team. This requires (7) _____ organisational, communication, problem-solving and research skills, in addition to a high degree of (8) _____, initiative and discretion.

TEND
GLAMOUR
IMMENSE
DEMAND
PROVIDE
PRESSURE
EXTEND
STAND
FLEXIBLE

READING

1 You are going to read an article about a chef who took part in a TV cooking show. Read the first paragraph of the text. What happens during the show?

EXAM TRAINING — READING AND USE OF ENGLISH PART 7

2 You are going to read an article about a chef who took part in a TV cooking show. Six paragraphs have been removed from the extract. Choose from the paragraphs A–G the one which fits each gap (1–6). There is one extra paragraph which you do not need to use.

Taking part in a REALITY TV COOKING SHOW

The premise of *Kitchen Talents*, which I recently took part in, is that ten professional chefs battle it out in a knock-out competition. Each episode, the 'executive' chef who heads the show presents participants with a challenge: to use a particular ingredient or create a vegan dish. This chef, along with a panel of judges, selects those who'll go on to cook again in the next round, with the weakest contestant leaving the competition.

1 ☐

These are welcomed with open arms by the victorious chef and there will be sceptics amongst the audience who believe that anyone who appears on TV is in it for financial gain or recognition. There's an element of that; chefs do want to climb the professional ladder. Generally, though, their motivation is to create better food.

2 ☐

It's said you never should, though, because they won't live up to expectations. Coming face-to-face with one of mine, however, – the executive chef – was not in the least disappointing. I was starstruck. That didn't last, as we contestants were plunged into our first test: to create our 'signature dish', one we'd feel comfortable putting before the judges.

3 ☐

A team of food critics, they were no less formidable in their commentaries than the executive chef. They gave praise where it was due and polished off the dishes they enjoyed. But at times I felt they hadn't understood what I'd been trying to achieve; at others, frustrated by my lack of ability to impress.

4 ☐

It's tough being on the receiving end of feedback like that, but standards can't slip in hospitality. I'd learned that the hard way as a young chef and it was a shock to the system being on the back foot again, my every move scrutinised. But if the chefs I'd previously worked under hadn't pointed out my errors, the thought of entering *Kitchen Talent* wouldn't have entered my mind.

5 ☐

That person was worthy of it and I was more relieved than anything: I wouldn't have to do the interviews I knew they'd be catapulted into. That isn't to say I didn't gain publicity for my restaurant. I'll be forever grateful to *Kitchen Talent* for raising my profile and giving me the opportunity to put everything I'd learned into practice.

6 ☐

The majority insisted I should've won and that was always a boost. Plus, restaurant bookings went through the roof for a while. My photo was plastered all over local social media. I was out of my comfort zone, but things have died down again now and I'm as anonymous as I ever was. That's fine by me!

A They were just doing their job, after all – the one I do in my own restaurant when I preside over an evening's service. I'm supportive of my sous chefs, but if a dish doesn't come up to scratch, I have to explain what went wrong and ask that it be started again.

B It was all I could do to supress my excitement and I had to keep the whole thing quiet until the show aired a few months later. In hindsight, I should've let everyone know so that once it was eventually broadcast, it wouldn't have had such an impact.

C And where else would you get the opportunity to do that alongside a top chef you've long admired? To be offered guidance from the executive chef and the judges is meaningful and inspiring. I couldn't wait to meet my heroes.

D My skills simply wouldn't have been up to it. Fortunately, they were, and I made it to the final. That spurred me on to do the best cooking I've ever done. Still, it was another participant who walked away with the trophy.

E As we set about making food we'd honed to perfection, I became very aware of the hovering cameras. The sense of awkwardness stayed with me throughout filming. I was willing to put up with it for the sake of my craft, though, and poured everything I had into my attempt to wow the judges.

F Ultimately, one person is crowned the winner, and this brings them considerable prestige. Alongside this, rewards include book deals and further opportunities to appear on TV.

G Of course, I didn't get away with it altogether. There was no end of people approaching me afterwards saying 'Weren't you on that cooking show?' I felt mixed emotions about this.

GRAMMAR
CLEFT SENTENCES

1 Choose the correct options to complete the sentences, A, B or C.

1 ___ the movie is so popular is largely due to great marketing.
   A Why   B The reason why
   C The reason what

2 ___ I'd hate about fame is people staring at me.
   A The reason why   B The thing
   C It is the thing

3 What people want ___ is when the band's new album will be released.
   A knowing   B know   C to know

4 ___ I did my first school play that I realised I wanted to be an actor.
   A When   B Not until   C It was when

5 ___ realise is how lonely fame can be.
   A Something people don't
   B What people aren't
   C It is something that people don't

6 ___ wants is to become an influencer.
   A It was my friend who   B All my friend
   C My friend only

2 Complete the text with one word in each gap.

When I was about ten and my brother was 13, he got given a leaflet at school about an audition for a film. ¹_____ was my parents who first suggested he should audition, because he loved drama. Well, ²_____ happened was he got the job – the lead role in a huge film! When it came out, all of a sudden he was famous. At first it was really weird because everyone knew who he was, but this soon became normal. The best thing ³_____ it is that I now get to go to film premieres and meet famous people. The annoying thing ⁴_____, everyone I meet is only interested in talking about him! ⁵_____ people want to know most is what he's really like, but to me he's just my brother. ⁶_____ he wants to do is act and he isn't really interested in the limelight. That's the reason ⁷_____ he doesn't use social media. He still lives with me and our parents (although we do have a bigger house now!) and says that the ⁸_____ people who know the real him are us.

3 Complete the cleft sentences with your own ideas.

1 The reason why I watch/listen to _____.
2 Something that would be good about being famous is _____.
3 It is clear that to find fame you _____.
4 The celebrities who are the most interesting _____.
5 What I like most about my favourite film is _____.

ELLIPSIS AND SUBSTITUTION

4 Underline the ellipsis or substitution in the sentences.

1 There were many celebrities at the film premiere, but I only recognised a few.
2 Can you share that photo you took of me? I want to send it to my sister.
3 They say he is the best actor in the film, but I'm not so sure he is.
4 I'm not sure I have the time to watch a film tonight but if I do, I'll call you.
5 I think Zain should audition for the band, but I don't think he will.
6 Do you like the new Kraze album? I think I liked their last one better.

5 Write the words that are missing or have been substituted under each sentence in Exercise 4.

6 Rewrite the sentences to make them shorter by using ellipsis or substitution.

1 I can't lend you my band T-shirt for the concert tonight because it's my only band T-shirt!
2 I think there is too much celebrity news online. I don't like to read all the celebrity news.
3 Lorie Latchel and Michaela Stoppard are in that new comedy I want to see. I think Lorie Latchel and Michaela Stoppard are very good actors.
4 I've never been to a film studio, but I'd love to go to a film studio.
5 If you don't want to come to the concert with me, then I am sure that Sam will come with me.

7 >>> **STRETCH!** Read the text. Rewrite the sentences in bold to use either a cleft sentence, ellipsis or substitution (or more than one of these).

¹Many people thought that when TV was invented TV would be the beginning of the end for radio.

_____

However, radio continued to be popular. ²Radio was still popular because people could listen in the car, while they were working or while busy doing other things.

_____

However, will the rise in the popularity of podcasts mean the end of radio? ³Many people think it will be the end of radio.

_____

⁴Podcasts are popular because you can choose what you listen to and when you listen to the podcasts.

_____

You can also find a huge number of podcasts on many different topics. ⁵People don't just listen to podcasts for entertainment, many people find podcasts are a great source of learning too.

_____

⁶People also like the fact they can 'binge listen' to a podcast by listening to many episodes in a row.

_____

So, with the rise of podcasts as well as the popularity of streaming music, will we finally see the demise of the radio?

VOCABULARY

ADJECTIVES ABOUT FAME

1 Complete the article with the adjectives in the box. Use each adjective only once.

> eccentric groundbreaking iconic
> infamous legendary mainstream obscure
> prestigious renowned short-lived

Last night saw the ¹ _____ Golden Notes Awards held at the Glenfield Ballroom, a venue which has become ² _____ for some of the most amazing concerts over the last century. All of the most famous and ³ _____ music stars in the country were there, including MelanieZ, who is known for her ⁴ _____ dress sense and arrived in a dress made entirely of feathers. The show opened with a performance from ⁵ _____ dance act T4T, who performed a series of tracks from their now ⁶ _____ first album. Isak Inole won the award for album of the year and artist of the year for his third album, proving the many people who thought his career would be ⁷ _____ after winning a TV talent show wrong.

Of course, the awards aren't just for ⁸ _____ acts, but also more ⁹ _____ musicians, with low-profile folk duo Deb & Dirk winning independent release of the year. Luckily, the awards passed without an incident like last year's now ¹⁰ _____ protest against AI in the music industry.

2 Answer the questions for you.

1 What is the most prestigious music award in your country?
2 Is there an renowned music venue in your city?
3 Do you prefer mainstream music or more obscure music?
4 Who is a legendary musician from your country? What is their most iconic album or song?
5 Who is the most eccentric musician or band from your country?

UNIT 9 THE FAME GAME | 79

LISTENING

1 You are going to listen to an interview in which two psychologists talk about fame. Which of the following topics might come up in their discussion?

1. people who did not expect to become famous
2. reasons for wanting to become famous
3. the impact of fame on a person
4. how being famous changes someone
5. the personality traits of people who seek fame

2 Read the questions in the exam task. Do they contain any ideas not mentioned in Exercise 1?

EXAM TIP

You should be able to divide the discussion in Part 3 into sections according to the order and topic of the questions. Listen to the whole section of the recording that corresponds to each question before choosing your answer.

3 Underline the key words in the questions and options. Try to predict the answers.

EXAM TASK LISTENING PART 3

4 🔊 9.1 You will hear an interview in which two psychologists called Robert Turnbull and Maria Muñoz are talking about fame. For questions 1–6, choose the answer (A, B, C or D) which fits best according to what you hear.

1 What does Robert explain about the kind of people who seek fame?
   A They do not fit a stereotype.
   B They seek fame for a number of reasons.
   C They can be unsure about what drives them.
   D They often do not start out hoping to become famous.

2 What does Maria do when answering the question about becoming a social media influencer?
   A explain the attitude people in other industries have towards influencing
   B make a negative comparison between influencing and other roles
   C justify why some people want to become influencers
   D issue a warning about what it takes to become an influencer

3 What do the speakers agree about how the meaning of celebrity has changed?
   A Some people are keen to reach celebrity status for any reason.
   B There are different ideas about what should constitute celebrity.
   C Many people in modern society become celebrities unintentionally.
   D Famous people today tend to be less talented than celebrities of the past.

4 According to Robert, when people become famous without meaning to, they may feel
   A keen not to draw any further attention to themselves.
   B surprisingly grateful for the opportunities it presents.
   C overwhelmed with the responsibility of behaving in a certain way.
   D unsure about what it was that resulted in them becoming famous.

5 When asked about how fame changes people, Maria believes that
   A it's impossible to reverse its psychological impact.
   B it's easy to become overly proud of one's status.
   C it's important to try to maintain a sense of self.
   D its benefits may be rather short lived.

6 When referring to the writer Oscar Wilde's quote, Robert reports feeling
   A surprised by the insight into what it means to be famous.
   B unhappy about some ways people try to become famous.
   C uncertain about his right to judge other people's aspirations.
   D amused by the author's skill at lightening tricky situations.

80 | UNIT 9 THE FAME GAME

WRITING

A FORMAL LETTER

1 Read the extract in the writing task. Do you agree with the opinion? Why? / Why not?

> You see this extract in an English-language magazine:
>
> 'Celebrities should use their fame to draw attention to good causes, such as preventing climate change, animal conservation, or health charities. They are best placed to encourage the general public to make changes and are more likely to have an impact than so-called experts.'
>
> Write a letter to the editor of the magazine, saying how you feel about the opinions expressed.

2 Read the exam task and answer the questions.
1. What kind of letter should you write (formal, neutral or informal)?
2. Who is the target reader of the letter?
3. What points should you include in your letter?

3 Complete the model answer with one word in each gap.

< Inbox   2 Messages   ∧ ∨

Dear Editor,

I recently read an article about celebrity in your magazine. One comment suggested that celebrities ought to highlight the work of charities and other organisations which strive to make the world a better place, and that they are in a good position to influence the public.

¹_____ I believe is that although it is true that being in the limelight means having the opportunity to speak out, I am not convinced that famous people are in the best position to tell others what they should do. What concerns me ²_____ that the majority are unlikely to be specialists in subjects like animal conservation, global warming or charity work. ³_____ of what celebrities usually do has nothing whatsoever to do with serious issues.

⁴_____ is respected, experienced members of the organisations in question who should be given a platform to voice their opinions, persuading others to take appropriate action. The reason ⁵_____ is that they are far more likely to be taken seriously. Unfortunately, our TV screens and magazines give too much coverage to those who are 'famous for being famous' rather than genuinely ground-breaking indivduals.

To sum up, it is ⁶_____ the people with real expertise who should be given the opportunity to speak out and appeal to the public, rather than so-called celebrities who have little to offer.

Yours sincerely,
Chandra Pandit

EXAM TIP

Remember to use appropriate language for a formal letter. For example, avoid using contractions, slang or colloquial language.

4 Read the exam task. Make notes on each point and plan the organisation of your letter.

✓ EXAM TASK   WRITING PART 2

You have been talking about fame in your English class and would like to get different perspectives on it. You would like to invite a local celebrity to give a talk about the positives and drawbacks of fame.

Write a letter to the celebrity, inviting them to give the talk, explaining what the students would like to know about and saying why coming to give the talk would be useful for both the students and the celebrity.

Write your **letter**. You do not need to include postal addresses.

5 Write your answer in 220–260 words in an appropriate style.

SELF-EVALUATION

Check your writing:

Content: Have you started and ended your letter properly and used an appropriate register throughout? ☹ 😐 😑 ☺

Communication: Have you communicated your ideas effectively and given reasons to support your answers? ☹ 😐 😑 ☺

Organisation: Is your letter well-organised and coherent? ☹ 😐 😑 ☺

Language: Have you used a range of vocabulary and grammatical structures accurately? ☹ 😐 😑 ☺

6 💼 **Digital Literacy** Your digital footprint is the trail you leave online: your posts on social media, things you like and your browsing history. Employers, colleges and universities might search for your footprint online. Would you be happy with what they found about you? Can you think of any celebrities that have got in trouble for their digital footprint?

INTERVIEW TECHNIQUES

Who would you interview if you could interview anyone? Why?
How would you feel about interviewing them?
Do you think it is easier to be interviewed or to be the person interviewing? Why?

1 USING INTONATION FOR EMPHASIS

Say the sentence pairs below, stressing the word in bold each time. How does the meaning change?

I **never** imagined my videos would become so popular.
I never imagined my **videos** would become so popular.

It takes **a lot** of time and effort to plan and make interesting content.
It takes a lot of time and effort to plan and make **interesting** content.

Take turns saying the sentences below to a partner, emphasising different words each time. How does your partner think the meaning changes?

I couldn't believe how many journalists were outside my house.
I didn't really think about becoming famous, I just wanted to do something I loved.
Something people don't understand about fame is just how hard it is to find people you can trust.
What I really want to do is start directing films as well as acting in them.

2 USING BODY MOVEMENTS DURING INTERVIEWS AND DISCUSSIONS

How would you feel during an interview or discussion if someone …
crossed their arms?
nodded their head?
leant forward in their chair?
leant back in their chair?
looked at their watch or phone?
raised their eyebrows?
rolled their eyes?
fidgeted?

Plan your interview

My group is: Me, _____ and _____.

We are roleplaying an interview with: _____

What we know about interviewee / topic _____ : _____
_____ _____ _____

My role is interviewee / interviewer / observer.

_____'s role is interviewee / interviewer / observer.

_____'s role is interviewee / interviewer / observer.

82 | UNIT 9 THE FAME GAME

3 USING OPEN AND CLOSED QUESTIONS

ORACY 5

Think of at least three open and three closed questions.

Open questions	Closed questions
What is your favourite type of cheese?	Do you like cheese?

What follow-up questions could you ask for the closed questions? Note down some ideas.

Reflections on the interview

Things that went well:
_____
_____

Things that could be improved:
_____
_____

How/When I used emphasis:
_____
_____

How I tried to use my movements:
_____
_____

Balance of open, closed and follow-up questions:
_____
_____

SELF-EVALUATION

I can ...
- use intonation for emphasis. ○
- use closed and open-ended questions appropriately. ○
- use body movements during interviews and discussions. ○
- role play an interview, asking for clarification and expanding on answers when necessary. ○

UNIT 9 THE FAME GAME | 83

REVIEW 3 UNITS 7–9

GRAMMAR 7

1 Choose the correct answers to complete the notice.

The Larkside Bay summer fair is this weekend. We ¹*manage to / are entitled to* close the High Street from 10pm on Friday until 10 pm on Saturday so we ²*are able to / are supposed to* set up and hold the fair. Cars ³*are free to / are banned from* the street between these times. If you park on the street, you ⁴*are able to / are required to* move your car on Friday evening. Residents ⁵*are free to / are supposed to* drive into and out until 8 am on Saturday, but after that time you will ⁶*be supposed to / be unable to* access your properties by vehicle.

All stallholders ⁷*are obliged to / managed to* be on site to set up their stalls by 8 am and visitors ⁸*are required to / are permitted to* enter the fair from 10 am.

We hope everyone has a great day and the rain ⁹*is allowed to / manages to* stay away!

2 Complete the sentences with the words in the box. Add the correct prepositions before and after the word.

> account ~~aid~~ behalf charge
> keeping line means return

1 The café is having a fundraising barbecue next week ___in aid of___ the local food bank.
2 I'm not sure that new apartment building is _____ the character of the town.
3 There's no Pilates class today _____ the hall being used for a council meeting.
4 We need a volunteer to be _____ the key to the tennis club gates.
5 The school will be updating its data protection _____ the latest government advice.
6 _____ the whole community, we would like to express our thanks to you.
7 There will be cakes available in the hall tomorrow _____ a small donation.
8 The first aid course will be taught _____ online learning and practical sessions.

3 Find and correct six errors in the text.

<u>Red Fire Warning from 6 am to 11 pm tomorrow</u>
Tonight there is a strict fire ban on account for the very hot weather and high winds expected tomorrow. Residents are not permitted light any fires between the hours stated above. This includes cooking by mean of open fires or barbecues. You are require to check your fire plan and you should supposed to prepare a bag in case you need to leave your property. In the line with advice from the fire brigade, residents should leave their property at the first sign of trouble.

VOCABULARY 7

1 Complete the sentences with community and belonging phrases.

1 Schools should always offer a s_____ e_____ to all its pupils.
2 Spending too much time online can lead to s_____ i_____.
3 It is better to live in a small, c_____-k_____ c_____ than in a big city.
4 Teenagers are normally more influenced by their p_____ g_____ than by their families.
5 It is better to have a f_____-t_____-f_____ i_____ when talking about serious topics.
6 Most people want to feel a s_____ o_____ b_____, not feel like an o_____.
7 Things that are a part of m_____ s_____ now would seem very strange to people from one hundred years ago.

2 Complete the sentences with the correct options. Then match the questions to the answers.

1 What *amenities / urban sprawl* do you have in your town?
2 What are the main issues around *green belt / overcrowding*?
3 How can we prevent *infrastructure / traffic congestion*?
4 What can city planners do to prevent *housing / urban sprawl*?
5 What things can city planners do to help with *urban renewal / amenities*?

a We can improve road and public transport *infrastructure / congestion*.
b There is a doctors surgery, a library, a post office and a supermarket.
c They can develop old buildings into *new overcrowding / housing* and businesses.
d It can affect people's quality of life, including both their physical and mental health.
e One of the best things cities can do is create a *green belt / urban renewal*.

GRAMMAR 8

1 Rewrite the active sentences in the passive.

1. They might give you a fine if you don't have a ticket.
   You _____.
2. He doesn't like people telling him what to do.
   He doesn't _____.
3. They want the court to give them time to appeal their prison sentence.
   They _____.
4. The headteacher isn't likely to accept our ideas about changing the uniform.
   Our ideas _____.
5. A big worry of mine is someone catching me in an online scam and losing all my money.
   Being _____.
6. We can refuse customers service if they don't pay in advance.
   Customers _____.

2 Put the words in the correct order to make passive sentences.

1. sent / were / a / we / bill / large
   _____
2. a / exam / us / maths / was / difficult / given / to
   _____
3. study / the / consider / students / given / their / options / to / a lot of / time / were
   _____
4. told / the / the / was / truth / court
   _____
5. homework / us / classes / more / than / ours / given / other / was / to
   _____
6. to / about / was / robberies / us / relayed / information / the
   _____

3 Rewrite the sentences in Exercise 2 to make different passive sentences.

1. *A large bill was sent to us.*
2. _____
3. _____
4. _____
5. _____
6. _____

VOCABULARY 8

1 Complete the podcast description with the correct form of the phrases in the box.

> break records   exceed expectations
> hamper progress   lead the way
> make headway   overcome an obstacle
> pursue a goal   rise to the challenge
> set a target   suffer a setback

Do you feel that no matter how many times you ¹_____, something always comes along to ²_____ or make you ³_____?
Well, have you ever considered that maybe you're stopping yourself from ⁴_____?
This podcast examines ways you can help yourself to ⁵_____ of achieving anything you want and ⁶_____ in the way of you achieving your dreams. You might even find that you ⁷_____ your own _____ about what you can achieve!
So, before you decide to ⁸_____, such as applying for a new job or changing career, have a listen. It has ⁹_____ for the most downloaded self-help podcast this year, so it ¹⁰_____ for people who want to find out how to help themselves.

2 Match the adverbs to the adjectives.

1. deadly   a grateful
2. deeply   b opposed
3. eternally   c positive
4. fully   d bizarre
5. overwhelmingly   e serious
6. strictly   f aware
7. strongly   g forbidden
8. utterly   h shocking

3 Complete the text with collocations from Exercise 2. There may be more than one possible answer.

We would like to inform the community that we are ¹_____ of the ²_____ claims that the town square is going to have a fast food restaurant built on it. As most of you know, building in the town square is ³_____ under current planning laws and we are ⁴_____ to changes to those. We found it ⁵_____ to find out that so many people believed the rumours.
You can be sure that we are ⁶_____ about public consultation regarding major changes in the town centre. We are ⁷_____ to everyone who responded to our last survey, which was ⁸_____ about the proposed changes to the indoor market.

REVIEW 3 UNITS 7–9

GRAMMAR 9

1 Complete the second sentence so that it has a similar meaning to the first.

1. I schedule my videos to upload every Tuesday.
   What I do _____.
2. I do that so that content is released regularly.
   The reason _____.
3. Subscribers like regular, consistent content.
   Something _____.
4. My tenth video went viral.
   It _____.
5. An influencer shared it, which helped the most.
   The thing _____.
6. She posted it on her stories.
   All _____.

2 Make each sentence shorter by either deleting or replacing any unnecessary words, or both.

1. Most young people would like to become famous, but not many of these young people will become famous.
2. People think that being famous is easy, but being famous isn't as easy as people think.
3. I don't think that actor is very good, but I know you think that actor is very good.
4. You're amazing at playing guitar. I wish I could play guitar as well as you play guitar.
5. I wanted to download a new album, but I already have enough albums.
6. I've got a projector for watching films now. You should get a projector too.

SELF-ASSESSMENT!

3 Look back at your work in Units 7–9.
- ☐ modal verbs
- ☐ complex prepositions
- ☐ passive extension and other passive forms
- ☐ passive verbs with two objects
- ☐ cleft sentences
- ☐ ellipsis and substitution

1. Tick ✓ the area of grammar that you feel most confident about.
2. Circle the area of grammar that you need to work on more.
3. Underline the area of grammar that you think you will use most in future.

VOCABULARY 9

1 Choose the correct answers to complete the sentences.

1. He won a sports scholarship to a university programme that has a lot of *scrutiny / prestige*.
2. My uncle should have gone into *show business / endorsements* as he loved performing.
3. I thought the *adulation / coverage* of the women's sports competition on TV was terrible.
4. My neighbour used to be famous, but now he lives in total *obscurity / notoriety*.
5. My grandad had a book of *autographs / stardom* from old film stars, but I couldn't read them!
6. I'd love to go on a reality TV show, but I couldn't bear the online *glamour / scrutiny*.

2 Match the adjectives in the box to the descriptions. You do not need to use all the adjectives.

> eccentric   groundbreaking   iconic
> infamous   legendary   mainstream   obscure
> prestigious   renowned   short-lived

1. This singer is very popular with people of all ages and their songs are often played on the radio. _____
2. This millionaire actor only ever wears green and lives in a caravan in the woods. _____
3. This musician had one hit single, but his album sold so badly that he faded back into obscurity. _____
4. It's the most famous and well-known award for literature in the world. _____

SELF-ASSESSMENT!

3 Look back at your work in Units 7–9.
- ☐ community and belonging
- ☐ urbanisation
- ☐ progress and achievement collocations
- ☐ adverb-adjective collocations
- ☐ fame

1. Tick ✓ the vocabulary group that you enjoyed learning about the most.
2. Circle the vocabulary group that you need to work on more.
3. Underline the vocabulary group that you think you will use most in future.

VOCABULARY REFERENCE 7–9

UNIT 7

close-knit community a group of people who know each other well and help and support one another
connectedness the feeling of being linked with others
disconnection a lack of association with others
face-to-face interaction physical communication between people
mainstream society the dominant group in a society, whose values and behaviours are considered typical
meaningful connections relationships that have a significant and positive impact on a person's life
outsider someone who does not belong to a particular group, organisation or place
peer group a group of people of about the same age or social position
sense of alienation the feeling of being isolated or disconnected from others
sense of belonging the feeling of being accepted and included in a group
social isolation the state of being separated from interactions and relationships
supportive environment a place where people are encouraged and helped by others
amenity a building, piece of equipment, or service that is provided for people's use, comfort or enjoyment
green belt an area of land around a city or town where no new building is allowed
housing buildings for people to live in
infrastructure basic systems, such as transport, that a country or organisation uses to work effectively
overcrowding containing too many people
traffic congestion the state of being full or blocked with traffic
urban renewal the improvement and replacement of areas or buildings in a city
urban sprawl the spread of a city into the area surrounding it, often without planning

UNIT 8

break records do something better than previously achieved
exceed expectations achieve a better result than expected
hamper progress prevent something or someone from advancing or developing
lead the way make more progress than others in something
make headway move forward or make progress
overcome an obstacle succeed in dealing with a problem preventing progress
pursue a goal take action to achieve something
rise to the challenge deal successfully with a difficult situation
set a target determine a particular number or amount of something that you want to attain or achieve
suffer a setback experience something that delays or prevents a process from developing
deadly serious not joking at all
deeply shocking extremely surprising, in a bad way
eternally grateful forever thankful
fully aware know completely about something
overwhelmingly positive almost completely good
strictly forbidden absolutely not allowed
strongly opposed completely against
utterly bizarre very weird

UNIT 9

adulation very great admiration or praise for someone
autograph a signature, especially of a famous person
coverage the reporting of an event or subject
endorsement publicly approving of a product or person
glamour the special, exciting and attractive quality of a person, place, or activity
notoriety the state of being famous for something bad
obscurity the state of not being known to many people
prestige respect and admiration given to someone or something for high quality, success, or social influence
scrutiny the careful, detailed and often excessive examination of something, often someone's private life
show business the entertainment business
stardom the quality of being famous, especially for entertaining people
the limelight attention from the public
eccentric behaving in a strange and unusual way
groundbreaking very new and different
iconic very famous or popular
infamous famous for something considered bad
legendary very famous and admired, especially relating to people or things in the past
mainstream considered normal or typical
obscure not known to many people
prestigious something respected for its importance
renowned famous for being or doing a particular thing
short-lived only lasting for a short time

DIGITAL CLASSROOM
PRACTICE EXTRA UNITS 7–9

EXPLORING EMPLOYABILITY 1

PROFESSIONAL DEVELOPMENT AND MANAGEMENT

1 THINK

1.1 Imagine yourself in a situation with a lot of challenging tasks to complete. Which of the following quotations do you think gives the most helpful advice?

1. Don't wish for **FEWER PROBLEMS**, wish for **MORE SKILLS**.

2. Your ability to **SET AND ACHIEVE GOALS** is perhaps the most **IMPORTANT SKILL** you can ever develop.

3. People are most creative when they care about their work and are stretching their skills.

4. I'm a big believer in always **CHALLENGING YOURSELF** and **LEARNING NEW SKILLS**.

2 ENGAGE

2.1 Watch the video in which Karem, a student nurse, talks to his mentor. Think about these questions.

1. How useful is this conversation for Karem? Why?
2. How often do you think Karem and Lucy should have this kind of conversation?

2.2 Watch the video again. Match the aspects of Karem's job 1–6 to what he says about them a–f.

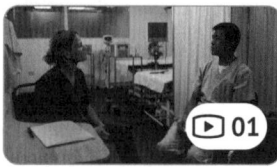

1. Paying attention to what patients say
2. Communicating with families
3. Giving injections
4. Noticing small changes
5. Learning about the technical side of nursing
6. Working as a theatre nurse

a. This is a goal for the future.
b. He recognizes he is often in too much of a hurry.
c. This is something he enjoys.
d. He thinks he can learn from his colleagues how to improve this.
e. He thinks he's made progress in this skill.
f. This is something he has become more confident about.

3 EXPLORE

3.1 Karem mentions the importance of learning by paying attention to what his colleagues are doing. Look at the skills described in 1–10. Which of them do you think you have? Which would you like to develop?

1. I've always been very organized – for example I put things back in the right place so I can always find them.
2. I listen to what others say and don't interrupt them unless I have to check or clarify something.
3. I anticipate how long a task is going to take but I know it might take less or more time depending on the circumstances.
4. No matter how confident I am about what I think, I always consider other people's ideas.
5. I keep notes and records even when things might seem unimportant or obvious.
6. I ask for other people's feedback on the tasks I have completed.
7. I'm always looking for new and better ways of doing things.
8. I regularly update my co-workers on what I am doing so we don't duplicate our work.
9. I am curious to know more about things people in my team do that are not my responsibility.
10. I make a point of deciding which order to do things, depending on how important they are.

3.2 Read comments a–j. Who could each speaker in Exercise 3.1 benefit from talking to?

a I focus on my tasks and let others get on with theirs.

b I fix time limits and stick to them.

c I know when my idea is the best, so I don't think I have to listen to anyone else in that situation.

d I often waste time because I leave stuff in a bit of a mess and am then not sure where things are.

e When I have a task, I like to get started ASAP, with no fixed sequence to follow.

f I get very impatient when people talk a lot and tend to finish their sentences for them.

g I like working in a team where we do our own thing and sort out any problems at the end of a task.

h I generally do things in the same way if they work.

i As long as I'm happy with my work, I don't ask people what they think of it.

j I only write down things I think are really significant.

(4) CREATE

4.1 You see the following advertisement and decide to apply for the position.

We are looking for summer course assistant to work with children between eight and 12. This is a demanding, full-time role perfect for someone who is energetic and responsible and enjoys working with children. A course assistant helps with indoor (arts and crafts, theatre, music etc) and outdoor activities (nature walks, sports, camping etc) and makes sure all the children are safe, participating and enjoying their summer course.

Make a list of the following:

1 Skills you already have you could use in this role.
2 Skills you think will improve and develop in this role.
3 New skills you would hope to learn in this role.

4.2 You get the position and have a great experience. Your manager tells you that in the future you could be a course director if you develop skills in the following areas:

a Managing financial accounts
b Communicating with parents
c Supporting and coordinating course assistants
d Arranging transport and day trips
e Providing support for children who feel sad because they are away from home
f Organizing catering to provide for special diets
g Resolving problems between children and resolving staff issues

Rank the skills from 1–10 according to how easy you feel it would be to for you to acquire these skills (10 = very confident, 1 = not confident at all).

4.3 Based on your answers to Exercise 4.2, make a list of your priorities to discuss in a meeting with your manager about the potential new role.

(5) REFLECT

1 To what extent did this unit help you think about the skills you would like to gain or improve?

2 In a situation like the one in Exercise 4.1, how confident are you that could clearly define and communicate your skills for a potential employer?

EXPLORING EMPLOYABILITY 2

COMMUNICATION

 **THINK**

1.1 Think of three situations you have experienced in the last two weeks when communication was necessary, for example in a shop, in class, with family or friends, asking for information, deciding what to do in your spare time, etc. Choose the best options 1–5 to describe the situations you are thinking of.

1. I expressed myself clearly and was understood.
2. I had some problems making myself understood.
3. I could have expressed myself better.
4. I achieved my objective.
5. I used some strategies I have learned/developed.

 **ENGAGE**

2.1 You have been given the option of doing a communication training session at work. Based on your answers to the previous exercise, which of the following do you think you would find useful?

① GETTING YOUR MESSAGE ACROSS
In this session you will learn how to get your ideas across to challenging audiences. You will get tips on making presentations, using persuasive language and adapting your message to the kind of audience you are talking to.

② TWO EARS, ONE MOUTH
There's an old saying that we should do 50% more listening than speaking, that's why we have two ears. But how can you make yourself into a better listener? This session will show you strategies and techniques to make you a better listener.

③ SENSE AND SENSITIVITY
In our multicultural societies we must recognize the fact that there are different ways of communicating based on culture and traditions. In this session we'll be looking at ways of making sure our interactions are respectful and successful.

④ INVESTING IN THE LANGUAGE BANK
Do you have the language you need to be an effective communicator? How can you build your resources and confidence by identifying the language you need? This session will give you ideas and advice for building a secure basis for projecting your ideas.

⑤ MUCH MORE THAN WORDS
Effective and productive communication comes about as a result of many factors apart from the words you use. Body language, tone and voice, turn-taking, showing interest – these are just some of the skills we need. This session will help you identify those areas where you can benefit from improving these skills.

2.2 Look at the comments below. Which sessions from Exercise 2.1 would each person benefit most from attending?

Miguel I worry that I might come across as too direct, even a bit rude. People from my part of country have a reputation for that, and it's not always seen as a positive thing.

Paula When I've given talks, I often get feedback from classmates who say I look nervous and don't make eye contact with the audience, which I guess is true. I am very shy. I'm a good writer so I know my ideas are clear, but I never get a really positive response.

Mira In discussions and debates I'm so focused on what I'm going to say and preparing my arguments that I sometimes lose track of what we're talking about. I really want to make a good impression, but I need some help to change my mindset.

Enzo We do a lot of presentations on my course, and I'm good at creating the visuals and even short, funny videos, but sometimes they work and sometimes they don't. I don't know why the same talk can be great with one group, but another finds it boring.

Lilly I know what I want to say, but I have a lot of doubts about the right way to express myself and which phrases are appropriate in different situations.

3 EXPLORE

3.1 Read the comments made after attending the sessions in Exercise 2.1. Which ones are they describing?

a I found it really useful to have a kind of checklist to refer to that's a way of not taking things for granted. A person's age or the country they grew up in can influence the productive conversations you can have. I think I'll be more aware of putting myself in someone else's shoes in the future.

b We did an exercise where we had to imagine our minds as completely empty and the only thing we could think about was what we could hear. I know it sounds a bit weird, but it helped a lot.

c I understand more now about 'reading the room,' or being aware of your audience and asking myself questions like 'Do they know a lot about this?', 'Would an ice-breaker make people relax?' and 'Would it be better if I stand closer to the people here?'

d There were lots of interesting theories, but the single most useful idea was actually really simple – make a video of myself and watch it to see how I can be more natural and avoid making mistakes.

e We looked at useful phrases for expressing ideas and focused on the idea of register – how your language changes depending on how formal or informal the situation is. That gave me some very helpful guidelines.

3.2 Which ideas mentioned in Exercise 3.1 could help you become a better communicator?

4 CREATE

4.1 You have been invited to attend two sessions from Exercise 2.1. Write a letter saying which sessions you have chosen, and why. Refer to the comments made by attendees in Exercise 3.1 and explain how you think the skills you will learn can help you in the future. Your letter should be between 250–300 words.

5 REFLECT

1. How important do you think it is to make a conscious effort to improve our communication skills?

2. How can we get helpful feedback about our communication strengths and weaknesses?

3. It is useful to watch online videos to see how effective communicators works. When watching, think about what makes the speakers good communicators. YouTubers, for example, have a very different style to TED talk speakers – when is one more appropriate than another?

EXPLORING EMPLOYABILITY 3

EMOTIONAL INTELLIGENCE

1 THINK

1.1 Look at the photos of people doing things together. For each picture, rank the following (5 = most important, 1 = least important) according to what you think successful collaboration in these situations depends on.

- Explaining your ideas
- Listening to others
- Being prepared to change your mind
- Telling people what to do
- Letting people make suggestions

2 ENGAGE

2.1 Look at the five situations below and choose your most likely thought or reaction, A or B.

1 Jane doesn't answer you when you say hello.
  A That's so rude.
  B Maybe she's thinking about something important and didn't notice me.
2 Andy (who is a really keen gamer) looks very tired.
  A He might be sleeping badly because he's worried.
  B He probably was probably up half the night playing video games.
3 Alan gave a presentation, and it wasn't good.
  A I'll tell him he should let someone else do it next time.
  B I'll tell him he should practise with me beforehand next time.
4 You are late preparing your part of a team project because you have been looking after a younger sibling.
  A You work through the night to finish it on time.
  B You explain the situation to your team and ask them for more time or help.
5 You recently started working for an agricultural company. You think a client might be breaking the law.
  A Do nothing – you are new, and you shouldn't create problems.
  B Get a colleague's advice on what to do.

2.2 Look at the situations in Exercise 2.1 again. Which skill or behaviour 1–5 could be useful in each one?

a Supporting someone who is under stress.
b Helping someone improve their performance.
c Not making quick decisions until you have considered other possibilities.
d Work as a team or group to find effective solutions.
e Sharing your worries or problems with others.

2.3 Look at the examples of what people might say in response to the situations in Exercise 2.1. How effective do you think they would be in helping people to talk about their situations: very effective, moderately effective or not very effective?

1. Jane, are you all right? You seem very distracted.
2. You look terrible Andy. Are you sick or just going to bed too late?
3. Don't be too hard on yourself. Let's look at what went wrong.
4. We're all working on this together, so it's really important you do your part on time.
5. As you're new here, if there's anything you want to talk about, my door is always open.

3.1 Emilia has recently started working for an agricultural company and thinks a client might be breaking the law. As her boss doesn't support her theory, she talks to her colleague Maya. Watch Part 1 of the video. Which of the following does Maya <u>not</u> do?

1. Gossip about their colleague Phil.
2. Invite Emilia to explain what's worrying her.
3. Offers to write the report with Emilia.
4. Tells Emilia she only has a little time to spare.
5. Agrees that people being dishonest is frustrating.

3.2 Watch Part 2 of the video. Are the following statements true or false?

1. It is not the first time Phil has disagreed with his staff.
2. Maya is going to write the report.
3. Maya thinks Mr Wilson will admit he is using fertiliser.
4. Emilia feels Maya has helped her with a complicated problem.
5. Emilia can ask Maya for help in the future.

3.3 Complete the description of emotional intelligence using the words in the box.

constructively   empathy   positive
resilience   self-awareness   support

Emotional intelligence is many things. Firstly, it means demonstrating ¹_____, something that involves reflection – asking yourself questions about how you feel, and what causes those feelings. It is also about acting with ²_____, having the confidence and determination to keep improving even when things don't go according to plan. With colleagues or classmates, it is important to show ³_____, trying to understand what others think and feel and how we can ⁴_____ each other. Change and uncertainty are things we must expect and be ready to deal with ⁵_____. Learning to accept and even enjoy such challenges depends a lot on ⁶_____ relationships and good communication.

4.1 Look again at the situations in Exercise 2.1. Write a dialogue based on one of the situations that uses emotional intelligence to help the person involved.

1. Which aspects of emotional intelligence did you focus on in your dialogue? Why?
2. Has this unit given you any new ideas about how to create better interactions with classmates or team members?
3. To what extend does being aware of emotional intelligence help someone becomes a better team member?

EXPLORING EMPLOYABILITY 4

DIGITAL LITERACY

1 THINK

1.1 How often do you use the following digital tools, either for studying, hobbies or doing things in your free time?

- AI searches
- AI images
- text editing/spell-check programmes
- text to voice tools
- data analysis tools
- fact checking
- image/photo editing
- price comparisons
- animation makers
- planners/organizers

1.2 If you were asked to comment on your experience of one of the above, which would you choose, and why? If you have never used any of them, which do you think could be most useful, and why?

2 ENGAGE

2.1 Read five people's answers to the questions in Exercise 1.2. Which tools do they comment on? Have you had any similar experiences to the ones described?

1 Of course, this is great when you want a really specific image – maybe for a presentation, or an illustration for something you've written. And it's fun! Sometimes I just ask for a totally weird or improbable picture – my sister flying to the moon on a cheese sandwich for example – but most of the time I only use it for schoolwork. It's important to be respectful though – to make sure the results aren't offensive in any way.

2 I only started using this recently. I wanted a way of revising for tests and exams that suited me better, as I find it easier to remember what I hear than what I read. You just have to select the information you want from a file or website and then select the voice, gender and accent you like. You've got to try some different ones – there was an Australian one I found hard to understand – but then I found this kind of international-style speaker, and she's perfect.

3 I wanted to use this mainly because I'd had such a great holiday. My plan was to create a book using some of the photos I took. My idea was to write descriptions or talk about what we did there. I thought this is great! It's free, at least for ten days, and surely I only need a few hours. But I soon realized that it wasn't really – they had a way of telling you could pay or not, but in fact it wasn't an option, because the 'free' versions were such low quality. They also said anything you created with the free version was their property. I felt cheated, to tell the truth, or tricked at the least. And then they started to send me offers and adverts – loads of them – and are still sending me things even now!

4 I find this really useful for everything from homework and deadlines, to making arrangements with my friends, checking birthdays, and organizing trips. Because a lot of my content is personal I made absolutely sure the information I add is private. My friends tell me I'm paranoid, but I just think it's common sense. I don't want some stranger to have access to my private life!

5 Of course we're always using this now. It's totally changed the way you do homework, conduct research if you're working on a group project, or preparing a talk, just to mention a few examples. I thought it was very helpful that our school arranged an open discussion event so that we could talk about what it means and how we should take advantage of this brilliant resource. All of us – students, teachers and parents – felt it was essential that we agree on what is and isn't the right way to use it.

2.2 Match the speakers 1–5 in Exercise 2.1 to the comments a–g. Two speakers have two comments.

a Sensitivity to others is important when generating material.
b Your personal details might be at risk in some situations.
c It's better to be safe than sorry.
d Digital resources have both fun and serious uses.
e Some online digital resource providers might try to exploit you.
f There are digital resources that fit your way of working.
g It's important to reach an agreement about how to use it.

3 EXPLORE

3.1 Match the sentence halves to make comments by interns about working with digital tools.

1 I've always been very interested in creating visualisations of data …
2 The funny thing was I actually found out …
3 I wasn't expecting the business to be …
4 When I was creating digital content my mentor …
5 I learned the importance of maintaining a personal relationship …

a … I knew much more about using the app than most of the people there, so they came to me for help.
b … so strict about online security, but our manager explained it's really important for our own protection.
c … so I quickly worked out how to use the programme to get great results.
d … taught me a lot about the importance of using language which is inclusive.
e … with clients and not relying totally on the technology.

4 CREATE

4.1 Using the notes below, write a review of a digital resource designed to help young people identify their potential skills and give advice when they make job applications. Use the ideas and comments in the Engage and Explore exercises in your review.

Write your review in 250–300 words.

- Secure and reliable
- Very detailed – lots of questions that make you think carefully about your goals
- Takes into account your personality and idea – not just your interests
- A bit too focused on the financial sector; fewer options for charities and NGOs
- Great advice on writing a CV
- Free version is very limited
- Option of 1–1 interview practice (expensive)

5 REFLECT

1 Do you feel you can make good decisions about which digital tools are most useful for you? Why? / Why not?
2 How important is it to check the digital resources you use respect your privacy?
3 Which kinds of digital skills do you think your future employers might consider most important?

VOCABULARY BUILDER

UNIT 1 MY VOCABULARY

Can you remember the vocabulary from Unit 1? Use the letters and the number of letters to help you.

EXPRESSING CHANGE

1. a _ _ _ _ _   t _   c _ _ _ _ _ _ _ _
   c _ _ _ _ _ _ _ _ _ _ _ _ _ (5,2,8,13)
2. b _ _ _ _ _   a _ _ _ _ _   d _ _ _ _ _ _ _
   c _ _ _ _ _ (5,5,1,8,6)
3. c _ _ _ _ _ _   b _ _ _ _ _
   r _ _ _ _ _ _ _ _ _ _ _ (6,6,11)
4. e _ _ _ _ _ _ _ _ _ _   g _ _ _ _ _
   c _ _ _ _ _ (10,1,7,6)
5. m _ _ _   f _ _ _ _   s _ _ _ _ (4,1,5,5)
6. m _ _ _   s _ _ _ _ _ _ _ _
   c _ _ _ _ _ _ (4,8,7)
7. m _ _ _   w _ _ _ _   t _ _   t _ _ _ _ (4,4,3,5)
8. r _ _ _ _ _   u _ _ _ _ _ _ _ _ (6,9)
9. s _ _ _   s _ _ _ _   b _ _   s _ _ _ _ _
   s _ _ _ _ (3,1,4,3,6,5)
10. s _ _ _ _ _   a _ _ _ _ _   f _ _ _
    s _ _ _ _ _ _ _ (5,5,4,7)
11. s _ _ _ _   t _ _   s _ _ _ _ (4,3,4)
12. u _ _ _ _ _ _ _ _ _   _   c _ _ _ _ _ _ _
    t _ _ _ _ _ _ _ _ _ _ _ _ _ (7,1,8,14)

PHRASAL VERBS

13. d _ _   a _ _ _ _   w _ _ _ (2,4,4)
14. f _ _   i _ _ _ _ (3,4)
15. h _ _ _ _   o _ _ _ (4,3)
16. l _ _   o _ _ (3,3)
17. p _ _ _ _   a _ _ _ _ (4,4)
18. r _ _ _ _   i _ (4,2)
19. r _ _ _ _ _ _ _   t _ (6,2)
20. s _ _ _ _ _ _   u _ (5,2)
21. w _ _ _ _   o _ _ (4,3)

VOCABULARY EXTENSION

1 Match the underlined words and phrases in the comments from graduate workers 1–7 to the defintions in the box.

1. 'I used to panic when I experienced a <u>setback</u>, but now I calmly look for ways to improve the situation.'
2. 'I've learned that ways of working are not <u>set in stone</u> and it's all right to change your approach.'
3. 'I'm happy to <u>take the initiative</u> – I'm good at coming up with <u>fresh ideas</u>.'
4. 'I don't <u>hold back</u> any more – I share my ideas and am not afraid of being wrong.'
5. 'I love <u>to ring the changes</u> and try out new things in my role. If they don't work, I go <u>back to basics</u> and try again.'
6. 'When something isn't working, I think, OK, <u>tear it up</u> and try again!'
7. 'I'm much better at planning – I start off with a clear <u>game plan</u> and <u>streamline</u> processes so that they are easy to manage.'

a problem that makes something happen later or more slowly than it should
be the first one to do something
completely reject an idea you developed
design something so that it can move as effectively and quickly as possible
do something in a different way in order to make it more interesting
give your attention to the simplest and most important matters
new and original thoughts
not do something
strategy
very difficult or impossible to change

2 Complete the text with one word in each gap.

When Mariana took over her failing family restaurant business after college, she decided to ¹_____ the changes by ²_____ up the way things were done. She had a clear game ³_____. The business had good reputation, but it had failed to move ⁴_____ the times, especially in terms of decoration and image, so intead of altering it ⁵_____ recognition, she kept the friendly atmosphere but did ⁶_____ with a lot of the old furniture and painted it warmer colours. Due to her lack of experience, she had one or two ⁷_____, but the changes she made quickly improved the business without having to lay ⁸_____ any employees.

→ YOUR TURN

3 Think of situations when you changed the way you did something or tried a new approach or strategy to a task. Find two more new words to describe those situations. Write them here, with a translation or a description of the meaning.

UNIT 2 MY VOCABULARY

Can you remember the vocabulary from Unit 2? Use the letters and the number of letters to help you.

BODY IDIOMS
1. g _ _ c _ _ _ _ f _ _ _ _ (3,4,4)
2. g _ o _ _ _ m _ h _ _ _ _ (2,4,2,4)
3. m _ _ _ _ m _ b _ _ _ _ b _ _ _ (4,2,5,4)
4. h _ _ _ _ _ c _ _ _ _ _ _ _ o _ h _ _ _ _ (4,1,6,2,5)
5. t _ _ _ _ _ m _ a _ _ (5,2,3)
6. g _ _ s _ _ _ _ _ _ _ _ _ o _ _ y _ _ _ c _ _ _ _ (3,9,3,4,5)
7. b _ _ _ m _ m _ _ _ _ (4,2,4)
8. p _ _ _ _ m _ b _ _ _ _ _ _ (4,2,6)
9. b _ _ _ m _ l _ _ _ (4,2,3)
10. b _ _ _ _ _ _ _ d _ _ _ _ m _ n _ _ _ (7,4,2,4)
11. g _ _ o _ _ o _ h _ _ _ _ (3,3,2,4)
12. p _ _ _ _ s _ _ _ _ _ _ _ _ _ b _ e _ _ (4,9,2,3)

HEALTH COLLOCATIONS
13. b _ _ _ _ _ m _ _ _ _ _ _ h _ _ _ _ _ _ (5,6,6)
14. s _ _ _ _ _ _ _ f _ _ _ _ _ c _ _ _ _ _ _ _ _ d _ _ _ _ _ _ _ (6,4,1,7,7)
15. m _ _ _ _ _ _ _ _ _ p _ _ _ _ _ _ _ a _ _ _ _ _ _ _ _ (8,1,8,8)
16. g _ _ p _ _ _ _ _ _ o _ e _ _ _ _ _ _ _ _ _ (3,6,2,8)
17. r _ _ _ _ _ _ _ t _ t _ _ _ _ _ _ _ _ (7,2,9)
18. h _ _ _ a _ _ _ _ _ _ _ s _ _ _ e _ _ _ _ _ _ _ (4,7,4,7)
19. r _ _ _ _ _ _ _ s _ _ _ _ _ _ l _ _ _ _ _ _ (6,6,6)
20. a _ _ _ _ _ p _ _ _ _ _ _ _ _ _ f _ _ _ _ (5,9,5)
21. b _ _ _ _ _ u _ m _ s _ _ _ _ _ _ _ (5,2,2,7)
22. r _ _ _ _ _ _ _ m _ _ _ _ _ _ a _ _ _ _ _ _ _ _ _ (7,7,9)
23. b _ i _ p _ _ _ _ h _ _ _ _ _ _ (2,2,4,6)

VOCABULARY EXTENSION

1 Match the underlined expressions and body idioms in the comments 1–7 to the words and phrases in the box.

1. 'As a rule of thumb, he has physiotherapy twice a month – often more during the winter.'
2. 'Our coach turned a blind eye to the fact I was slower than usual, as she knew I was still recovering from injury.'
3. Because they are in the public eye, sports people should follow a healthy diet.
4. When the team came down with food-poisoning, Alix pointed the finger at the local café and refused to set foot in the place again.
5. My brother is a pain in the neck about training – he goes to the gym every day!
6. She lost her head and made a very dangerous tackle. Fortunately the other player wasn't hurt.
7. The doctor says my tennis injury is in my hands, so I've got to let it heal until the summer.

```
acted irrationally/irresponsibly
always in the news
as a general rule
blamed
go there
my responsibility
pretended not to notice
annoying
```

2 Choose the correct option, A, B or C, to complete the text.

Getting the support you need

You've probably been told how important it is to ¹_____ a positive attitude when you are recovering from a serious illness, which is why emotional support from friends and family is essential. This support helps ²_____ stress levels and ³_____ your mental health. Be aware though, that this can get out of ⁴_____ if people won't leave you alone! However, even if you're being a pain in the ⁵_____, those close to you will probably turn a ⁶_____ eye to your behaviour. As a rule of ⁷_____, honesty is the best policy in order to get the support you need. In many ways, it's in your ⁸_____ – you have to ask for what you need.

1. A run B maintain C extend
2. A reduce B drop C fall
3. A reach B grow C boost
4. A step B hand C reach
5. A arm B throat C neck
6. A closed B blind C quick
7. A thumb B hand C finger
8. A grip B fingers C hands

→ YOUR TURN

3 Find two more new words related to health. They might be related to your health or people you know or aspects of health you have studied. Write them here, with a translation or a description of the meaning.

UNIT 3 MY VOCABULARY

Can you remember the vocabulary from Unit 3? Use the letters and the number of letters to help you.

DESCRIBING FOOD

1. b _ _ _ _ (5)
2. c _ _ _ _ (5)
3. cri _ _ _ (6)
4. cru _ _ _ (6)
5. g _ _ _ _ _ (6)
6. i _ _ _ _ _ _ _ (8)
7. m _ _ _ _ _ _ (7)
8. m _ _ _ _ _ _ _ _ _ _ _ _ (13)
9. s _ _ _ _ _ _ (7)
10. s _ _ _ _ (5)
11. t _ _ _ _ _ (6)
12. u _ _ _ _ _ _ _ _ _ _ _ (12)

PHRASAL VERBS: EATING AND DRINKING

13. g _ _ _ d _ _ _ (4,4)
14. p _ _ _ a _ (4,2)
15. wa _ _ d _ _ _ (4,4)
16. wo _ _ d _ _ _ (4,4)
17. p _ _ _ _ _ o _ _ (6,3)
18. wa _ _ u _ (4,2)
19. wh _ _ u _ (4,2)
20. f _ _ _ _ d _ _ _ (5,4)
21. t _ _ _ i _ _ _ (4,4)
22. c _ _ o _ _ (3,3)

VOCABULARY EXTENSION

1 Read part of an interview with author about her new book (I = interviewer, M = Maya). Would you be interested in reading this book? Why? / Why not?

I: Maya, in *Eating Today*, you talk a lot about how the way we eat has changed in recent years. Is this a good thing?

M: I don't think it's good or bad, just different. What's certain is that we have a lot of choices, from <u>buffet</u> breakfasts to a <u>sharp increase</u> in home delivery options that are <u>dropped off</u> whenever you want. Shops <u>stock</u> a lot more foods from other countries, too.

I: You also write about food safety. What does that mean?

M: Many things. Are <u>regulations</u> being followed? <u>Hygiene</u> is so important in relation to food preparation. Also, how is food cooked? In Canada, for example restaurants are prohibited from serving <u>rare</u> steaks. I'm equally fascinated by the science and the psychology of food. How do our <u>taste-buds</u> work? Why do most of us have a favourite <u>comfort food</u>? So many interesting questions.

I: And do you like cooking?

M: Actually, I don't. My friends joke that my <u>speciality</u> is a cheese sandwich.

2 Match the underlined words and phrases in Exercise 1 to the definitions 1–10.

1. a sudden, large rise
2. meat that has only been cooked for a short time
3. degree to which something is kept clean, especially to prevent disease
4. take something to a particular place
5. the cells on your tongue that allow you to taste different foods
6. a meal where people serve themselves different types of food
7. type of food that people eat when they are sad or worried
8. have goods for people to buy
9. an official rule or the act of controlling something
10. something you are very good at

3 Write your answers to the following questions.

1. Which food do you find moreish? Is it your comfort food?
2. Which food do you tend to force down, but eat because it's good for you?
3. Do you or anyone in your family have a recipe they are famous for?
4. Can you name a shop that stocks a wide range of food?
5. Have you noticed a sharp increase in the popularity of any particular food recently?
6. Do you think people eat more when they have a buffet lunch or breakfast? Why? / Why not?

→ YOUR TURN

4 Find two more new words related to food. They might be related to the kinds of food you like or your typical diet. Write them here, with a translation or a description of the meaning.

UNIT 4 MY VOCABULARY

Can you remember the vocabulary from Unit 4? Use the letters and the number of letters to help you.

FRIENDSHIP

1 b _ _ _ _   g _ _ _ _ _ _ (4,1,6)
2 d _ _ _ _   a _ _ _ _ (5,5)
3 e _ _ _ _ _   y _ _ _ _   o _ _   c _ _ _ _ _ _ _ (5,4,3,7)
4 g _   b _ _ _ _   l _ _ _ _   w _ _ (2,4,1,4,3)
5 h _ _ _ _   u _ _   a _ _ _   d _ _ _ _ (3,3,5)
6 h _ _   i _   o _ _ (3,2,3)
7 _ s _ _ _ _ _ _ _ _ _   t _   c _ _ _   o _ (1,8,2,3,2)
8 r _ _   y _ _   u _   t _ _   w _ _ _ _   w _ _ (3,3,2,3,5,3)
9 s _ _ _ _ _ _   u _ _   f _ _ _ _ _ _ _ _ _ _ (6,2,1,10)
10 t _ _ _ _   a _ _ _ _ _   s _ _ _ _ _ _ _   b _ _ _ _ _   t _ _ _ _ _   b _ _ _ (4,5,7,6,5,4)

PERSONALITY TRAITS

11 c _ _ _ _ _ _ _ (7)
12 i _ _ _ _ _ _ _ _ _ _ (10)
13 l _ _ _ -b _ _ _ _ (4,4)
14 o _ _ _ _ _ _ _ _ (8)
15 r _ _ _ _ _ _ _ _ (8)
16 s _ _ _ _ _ _ _ _ _ (9)
17 s _ _ _ -a _ _ _ _ _ _ _ (4,7)
18 s _ _ _ -c _ _ _ _ _ _ _ _ _ (4,9)
19 s _ _ _ _ _ _ _ (7)
20 u _ _ _ _ _ _ _ (7)

VOCABULARY EXTENSION

1 **Look at this article from an online magazine. Which comments remind you of your friends?**

We asked people to tell us about someone whose friendship they value greatly, and why. Here are some of the answers:

1 Emma's particularly <u>good-natured</u> and always tries to help me when I have problems.
2 My friend Javier is so <u>courageous</u> – he never lacks bravery, whatever the situation.
3 Dana's a <u>people person</u> – she creates a really friendly atmosphere when we're in a group.
4 My mate Alex thinks <u>sensibly</u> and always tells me if I'm making a mistake or being <u>naïve</u>.
5 Angela can be a bit <u>distant</u>, and sometimes acts like she <u>couldn't care</u> less about our friendship.
6 Jenny likes lively conversations, so I have to be <u>alert</u> when I'm talking to her – when she <u>holds an opinion</u>, she's quick to defend it.
7 I truly value Omar's friendship. He's so <u>constant</u> – he never lets me down.

2 **Find five underlined words or phrases in Exercise 1 that mean the same as 1–5.**

1 to believe something
2 focused
3 very sociable
4 responsibly
5 innocent

Find five underlined words or phrases in Exercise 1 that mean the opposite of 6–10.

6 changeable
7 approachable
8 very concerned
9 unkind
10 cowardly

3 **Complete the text about a friendship with one word in each gap.**

They say the difference between family and friends is that you get to choose your friends but I don't ¹ _____ that opinion. I don't feel I 'chose' Simon. We just ² _____ it off immediately, as if he'd always been there, like family. That doesn't mean he's not very annoying at times – he's so ³ _____ -back that you can't get him to plan anything. And he has a kind of 'I couldn't ⁴ _____ less' attitude when there are problems that's really frustrating. He can be sarcastic, and cynical and tends to ⁵ _____ people up the wrong way, I think it's true to say he's not really a people ⁶ _____ , but none of that matters to me as he's totally loyal and reliable. Many relationships have their ups and ⁷ _____ , but ours has been one steady journey since we struck ⁸ _____ our friendship. He's kind and would never talk about you ⁹ _____ your back. If he has anything to say, he'll tell you directly and sincerely. I'm fortunate to have him as a friend.

→ YOUR TURN

4 **Find two more new words related to friendship. Write them here, with a translation or a description of the meaning.**

UNIT 5 MY VOCABULARY

Can you remember the vocabulary from Unit 5? Use the letters and the number of letters to help you.

EXPRESSIONS ABOUT TIME

1. b _ _ _ _ _   t _ _   t _ _ _ _ (6,3,5)
2. c _ _ _ i _ _ d _ _ (4,2,1,3)
3. f _ _   g _ _ _ (3,4)
4. f _ _   t _ _   t _ _ _   b _ _ _ _ (3,3,4,5)
5. h _ _ _   t _ _ _ _   o _   y _ _ _   h _ _ _ _ (4,4,2,4,5)
6. i _ _   f _ _ _ _ _ (2,1,5)
7. i _   t _ _   n _ _ _   o _   t _ _ _ (2,3,4,2,4)
8. k _ _ _   t _ _ _ (3,4)
9. l _ _ _   t _ _ _ _ _   o _   t _ _ _ (4,5,2,4)
10. m _ _ _ _   w _ _ _ _   t _ _   t _ _ _ _ _ (4,4,3,5)
11. o _   t _ _   s _ _ _ _   o _   t _ _   m _ _ _ _ _ (2,3,4,2,3,6)
12. o _ _ _   i _   b _ _ _ _   m _ _ _ (4,2,1,4,4)

MULTI-WORD VERBS: TIME

13. c _ _ _ _ _   u _   o _ (5,2,2)
14. b _ _ _ _   f _ _ _ _ _ _ _ (5,7)
15. d _ _ _   o _ (4,2)
16. f _ _   i _ (3,2)
17. f _ _   b _ (3,2)
18. h _ _ _ _   u _ (4,2)
19. l _ _   b _ _ _ _ _ _ (3,6)
20. r _ _ _ _   a _ _ _ _ _ _ _ (4,6)

VOCABULARY EXTENSION

1 Read the summary of a time management guru's podcast. What do you think of her ideas?

'A big mistake people make is having a 'wait and see', approach to time management. Even if you are not sure if something is going to happen, assume it is, and find time for it in your schedule. Don't be too ambitious at first. Plan the essentials and add more things later – a step-by-step approach works best. An improvement in your way of working is only a matter of time once you get started. If you rush into managing your time you risk creating stress. Time management will benefit you most when you're working round the clock and have a clear set of tasks. An allocation of priorities will help keep you on the ball, and consequently feel more positive about demanding work and deadlines. And give yourself a bit of flexibility – maybe you exceed the time limit you set yourself, or perhaps a simple task turns out to be more time-consuming than expected. Such things are a matter of course and don't mean you have failed. Part of organizing your time effectively involves anticipating change. It is a timeless truth that you should always expect the unexpected.'

2 Match the underlined words and phrases in Exercise 1 to the definitions 1–10.

1. a usual part of the way in which things are done and is not special
2. do something without deciding if you really want to do it
3. something that doesn't change as time passes
4. when you think that something will happen at some point in the near future
5. happening or done all day and all night
6. dealing with things in a fixed order
7. wait to discover what will happen
8. be greater than a number or limit
9. have all the latest information about a subject or activity and be able to do it well
10. something that takes a lot of time to do

3 Match questions 1–6 with the responses a–f.

1. Was it very time consuming?
2. He's getting too old to play professional football, do you think he will call it a day?
3. I heard they brought forward the operation, is that true?
4. Why did the meeting drag on so long?
5. It was such a boring concert!
6. I wonder if the café will move with the times and start doing take-away.

a. Yes, and just in the nick of time. She was feeling awful.
b. Eventually, maybe, but not for the time being. It's really behind the times.
c. Do you think so? For me the time flew by.
d. They had a lot of business to catch up on.
e. Of course, it's just a matter of time.
f. Not at all, we did it in a flash.

➡ YOUR TURN

4 Think of situations when time has been important for you either for good or bad reasons. Find two more new words to describe those situations. Write them here, with a translation or a description of the meaning.

UNIT 6 MY VOCABULARY

Can you remember the vocabulary from Unit 6? Use the letters and the number of letters to help you.

MULTI-WORD VERBS: COMMUNICATION

1 a _ _ _ _ _ s _ _ _ _ _ _ _ b _ _ (6,7,4)
2 b _ _ _ _ s _ _ _ _ _ _ _ _ _ _ o _ _ (5,9,3)
3 c _ _ _ _ a _ _ _ _ _ _ a _ (4,6,2)
4 g _ _ s _ _ _ _ _ _ _ _ _ a _ _ _ _ _ (3,9,6)
5 l _ _ _ s _ _ _ _ _ _ _ i _ o _
   s _ _ _ _ _ _ _ _ _ (3,7,2,2,9)
6 s _ _ _ _ o _ _ (5,3)
7 t _ _ _ _ s _ _ _ _ _ _ _ i _ _ _
   s _ _ _ _ _ _ _ _ _ (4,7,4,9)
8 t _ _ _ _ s _ _ _ _ _ _ _ o _ _ o _
   s _ _ _ _ _ _ _ _ _ (4,7,3,2,9)
9 t _ _ _ _ s _ _ _ _ _ _ _ _ _ o _ _ _
   w _ _ _ s _ _ _ _ _ _ (4,9,4,4,7)
10 g _ o _ a _ _ _ _ s _ _ _ _ _ _ _ _ _ (2,2,5,9)

BODY LANGUAGE IDIOMS AND VERBS

11 r _ _ _ _ _ e _ _ _ _ _ _ _ _ (5,8)
12 b _ _ _ y _ _ _ t _ _ _ _ _ _ (4,4,6)
13 s _ _ _ _ y _ _ _ s _ _ _ _ _ _ _ _ (5,4,9)
14 r _ _ _ y _ _ _ _ e _ _ _ (4,4,4)
15 s _ _ _ _ _ _ _ y _ _ _ h _ _ _ (7,4,4)

VOCABULARY EXTENSION

1 **Match the underlined words and phrases in the conversations with the defintions 1–8.**

Conversation 1

Dale So, how did you get on with Maria?

Ana Very well, although, she was a bit shy at first.

Dale Really? She seemed very <u>chatty</u> to me. She was so confident in that talk about learning sign language. The phrases she <u>kicked off</u> with, comparing how things are signed to spoken English, were really cool.

Ana She definitely <u>put forward</u> some interesting theories about how and why sign language originated. It was a very <u>smooth</u> presentation overall.

Conversation 2

Sara I thought the week was a great success. But it was a lot of work for us, don't you think?

Alan Absolutely. <u>Off the record</u>, I think we should have had extra staff to help organize the events.

Sara That's a <u>hot topic</u>, because some locals felt they weren't invited to participate. Jenny doesn't <u>beat about the bush</u>, and she told me she was annoyed.

Alan Yes, I don't understand why she wasn't on the committee – she knows the town <u>inside out</u> and gives history tours in her free time.

1 a subject that people discuss and have strong feelings about
2 begin
3 express yourself in a very indirect way
4 happening without problems or difficulties
5 in detail
6 talkative
7 say something you do not want repeated to other people
8 state an idea or opinion so that it can be considered or discussed

2 **Complete the story extract with words and phrases from Unit 6.**

We hadn't seen each other for years and Charlie suddenly wanted to let me in [1]_____ a secret. 'You're a journalist,' he said, 'so this is [2]_____ the record.' I told him he could trust me. He shrugged his [3]_____, 'Maybe I can, maybe I can't, but I have to tell someone,' he insisted. 'Do you remember that time we all went to the archaeology museum at school?'. I did. He'd talked us [4]_____ going because he was passionate about Egyptian history at the time. He kept going [5]_____ about the exhibitions. In fact, he came [6]_____ as a bit obsessed, and – well, not to beat [7]_____ the bush – we though he was a little crazy about his new interest. But we always did stuff together, so despite some [8]_____ eyebrows, we met one Saturday morning outside the museum. Charlie said he'd been studying the way pictures and symbols were used to get ideas [9]_____ and how for ages nobody knew what they meant. 'Well, that night, after going to the museum, I had *the* idea, the one that made me famous.' He paused. 'Come on!' I said. 'Blurt it [10]_____! Now you have to tell me what the secret is.'

> **YOUR TURN**
>
> 3 **Find two more new words related to language and communication. Write them here, with a translation or a description of the meaning.**

UNIT 7 MY VOCABULARY

Can you remember the vocabulary from Unit 7? Use the letters and the number of letters to help you.

COMMUNITY AND BELONGING

1 c _ _ _ _ -k _ _ _ _   c _ _ _ _ _ _ _ _ _ (5-4,9)
2 c _ _ _ _ _ _ _ _ _ _ _ _ _ (13)
3 d _ _ _ _ _ _ _ _ _ _ _ _ _ (13)
4 f _ _ _ _ -t _ -f _ _ _ _   i _ _ _ _ _ _ _ _ _ _ _ _ _ _ (3-1-3, 11)
5 m _ _ _ _ _ _ _ _ _ _   s _ _ _ _ _ _ _ (10,7)
6 m _ _ _ _ _ _ _ _ _ _   c _ _ _ _ _ _ _ _ _ _ _ _ (10, 12)
7 o _ _ _ _ _ _ _ (8)
8 p _ _ _   g _ _ _ _ _ (4,5)
9 s _ _ _ _   o _   a _ _ _ _ _ _ _ _ _ _ (5,2,10)
10 s _ _ _ _ _   o _   b _ _ _ _ _ _ _ _ _ (5,2,9)
11 s _ _ _ _ _   i _ _ _ _ _ _ _ _ _ (6,9)
12 s _ _ _ _ _ _ _ _ _ _   e _ _ _ _ _ _ _ _ _ _ _ (10,11)

URBANISATION

13 a _ _ _ _ _ _ _ (7)
14 g _ _ _ _ _   b _ _ _ _ (5,4)
15 h _ _ _ _ _ _ _ (7)
16 i _ _ _ _ _ _ _ _ _ _ _ _ _ _ (14)
17 o _ _ _ _ _ _ _ _ _ _ _ _ (12)
18 t _ _ _ _ _ _ _   c _ _ _ _ _ _ _ _ _ _ (7,10)
19 u _ _ _ _   r _ _ _ _ _ _ _ (5,7)
20 u _ _ _ _   s _ _ _ _ _ _ (5,6)

VOCABULARY EXTENSION

1 Look at this extract from a magazine article. Who do you think misses where they used to live most?

1 Many residents of Redfield, a London borough, have left their homes due to <u>steep rises</u> in rent and property prices, with some forced to move to <u>the back of beyond</u>. We asked what they miss about their old neighbourhood.

2 'The people. We didn't always see <u>eye to eye</u>, but you could <u>share your problems</u> when you needed to.'

3 'Frankly, not much! The house we lived in was <u>in ruins</u>, so when they got <u>planning permission</u> to rebuild the street, we decided to move.'

4 'The sense of community. It was to our <u>mutual advantage</u> to make sure the neighbourhood was safe and people were <u>unselfish</u> when it came to helping each other.'

5 'The elderly social centre. Nobody has <u>taken the initiative</u> to start one here. You're very much on your own and there's nobody to give you a <u>helping hand</u> when you need one.'

2 Match the definition pairs a–e from Exercise 1 with the underlined words and phrases in 1–5.

a when something benefits two people or groups / when a person thinks about what is good for other people
b have the same opinions / talk to someone when you have difficulties/
c when a building is extremely badly damaged / legally allowed to build
d a big increase / a place far away from any big town
e to be the first one to do something / provide assistance

3 Choose the correct option, A, B or C, to complete the text.

There are many reasons why people might want to leave a city, for example traffic [1] _____ or the consequences of [2] _____. But the fact is we are living in the time of megacities, when [3] _____ sprawl often invades what is intended to be a [4] _____ belt, and areas that shouldn't receive [5] _____ permission become new neighbourhoods. What is obvious is that people living in large new developments often suffer from a [6] _____ of isolation. It takes time to build communities and make [7] _____ connections. It's also harder to keep in touch with your [8] _____ group and extended family, which results in a steep [9] _____ in loneliness. Megacities might have the advantage of offering work and amenities, but urban planners have a responsibility to [10] _____ the initiative and create communities.

1 A complication   B congestion   C completion
2 A over-crowding B over-paying C overrating
3 A urbanised   B urbane   C urban
4 A safe   B green   C closed
5 A growing   B built   C planning
6 A sense   B sensibility C sensation
7 A memorable   B meaningful   C manageable
8 A friend   B peer   C close
9 A raise   B rise   C rising
10 A take   B make   C do

➡ YOUR TURN

4 Find two more new words related to community. Write them here, with a translation or a description of the meaning.

UNIT 8 MY VOCABULARY

Can you remember the vocabulary from Unit 8? Use the letters and the number of letters to help you.

PROGRESS AND ACHIEVEMENT COLLOCATIONS

1 b _ _ _ _   r _ _ _ _ _ _ _ (5,7)
2 e _ _ _ _ _   e _ _ _ _ _ _ _ _ _ _ _ _ (6,12)
3 h _ _ _ _ _   p _ _ _ _ _ _ _ (6,8)
4 l _ _ _   t _ _   w _ _ (4,3,3)
5 m _ _ _   h _ _ _ _ _ _ _ (4,7)
6 o _ _ _ _ _ _ _ _   a _   o _ _ _ _ _ _ _ _ (8,2,8)
7 p _ _ _ _ _ _   g _ _ _ (6,1,4)
8 r _ _ _   t _   t _ _ _   c _ _ _ _ _ _ _ _ _ (4,2,3,9)
9 s _ _   _   t _ _ _ _ _ (3,1,6)
10 s _ _ _ _ _   s _ _ _ _ _ _ _ (6,1,7)

ADVERB-ADJECTIVE COLLOCATIONS

11 d _ _ _ _ _   s _ _ _ _ _ _ (6,7)
12 s _ _ _ _ _ _ _ _   f _ _ _ _ _ _ _ _ (8,9)
13 f _ _ _ _   a _ _ _ _ (5,5)
14 s _ _ _ _ _ _ _ _   o _ _ _ _ _ _ _ (8,8)
15 d _ _ _ _ _   s _ _ _ _ _ _ _ (6,8)
16 e _ _ _ _ _ _ _ _ _   g _ _ _ _ _ _ _ (9,8)
17 u _ _ _ _ _ _ _   b _ _ _ _ _ _ _ (7,7)
18 o _ _ _ _ _ _ _ _ _ _ _ _ _   p _ _ _ _ _ _ _ _ (14,8)

VOCABULARY EXTENSION

1 Read the interview with an inventor of a system which reduces the risk of malaria (I = interviewer, J = Jan). What obstacles did he face?

I: So Jan, I think it's true to say a lot of people thought your idea of a tube to catch mosquitos was crazy.

J: Absolutely, I visited a lot of towns and talked to builders ¹ with a view to incorporating my system into their houses. But it was hard to convince them, which I understand. You have to take things ² step by step and demonstrate that your idea really works.

I: And is that what happened?

J: In time, yes. The people I spoke to were ³ clearly determined to find solutions to this problem.

I: Tell me a bit about how you came up with the idea.

J: I ⁴ drew on my experience as an engineer and ⁵ deepened my understanding of how malaria spread, that's all.

I: That's very modest! It was ⁶ truly brave of you to give up a secure job to focus on your idea without knowing if it was going to work.

J: Giving up my job was actually ⁷ the push I needed – I had to make it work as my family was depending on me.

I: Well, no doubt your invention is one of ⁸ the summits of your career, so congratulations.

2 Match the underlined words and phrases 1–8 in Exercise 1 to the words and phrases in the box.

> extend   have great courage
> it was my aim   motivation
> point of maximum success
> really focused on achieving something
> slowly   use or refer to

3 Write your answers to the following questions.

1 How good are you at doing things step by step?
2 What subject would you like to deepen your knowledge of?
3 Can you think of a skill you were able to draw on recently to solve a problem?

4 Complete the report below with words from Unit 8.

School vegetable garden project

As you will be ¹ _____ aware, our school definitely ² _____ the way with its garden project initiative, as several others have introduced similar schemes. While the progress this year has been ³ _____ positive, we must recognise that we ⁴ _____ ourselves unrealistic targets. Bad weather ⁵ _____ our progress but the team ⁶ _____ to the challenge by doing extra work at the weekends. The tomato plants in particular ⁷ _____ expectations and we produced almost 50% more than last year. We also introduced some new plants – including carrots and beans – so we really ⁸ _____ headway at creating greater variety. We are ⁹ _____ determined to expand the project with a ¹⁰ _____ to making it a popular activity with students. This long term plan will develop step by ¹¹ _____.

→ YOUR TURN

5 Think of situations when you feel you made progress or faced challenges. Find two more new words to describe those situations. Write them here, with a translation or a description of the meaning.

VOCABULARY BUILDER | 103

UNIT 9 MY VOCABULARY

Can you remember the vocabulary from Unit 9? Use the letters and the number of letters to help you.

FAME

1. a _ _ _ _ _ _ _ _ (9)
2. a _ _ _ _ _ _ _ _ (9)
3. c _ _ _ _ _ _ _ (8)
4. e _ _ _ _ _ _ _ _ _ _ (11)
5. g _ _ _ _ _ _ (7)
6. n _ _ _ _ _ _ _ _ (9)
7. o _ _ _ _ _ _ _ _ (9)
8. p _ _ _ _ _ _ _ (8)
9. s _ _ _ _ _ _ _ (8)
10. s _ _ _ b _ _ _ _ _ _ _ (4,8)
11. s _ _ _ _ _ _ (7)
12. t _ _ l _ _ _ _ _ _ _ _ _ (3,9)

ADJECTIVES ABOUT FAME

13. e _ _ _ _ _ _ _ _ (9)
14. g _ _ _ _ _ _ _ _ _ _ _ _ _ (14)
15. i _ _ _ _ _ (6)
16. i _ _ _ _ _ _ _ (8)
17. l _ _ _ _ _ _ _ _ (9)
18. m _ _ _ _ _ _ _ _ _ (10)
19. o _ _ _ _ _ _ (7)
20. p _ _ _ _ _ _ _ _ _ _ (11)
21. r _ _ _ _ _ _ _ (8)
22. s _ _ _ _ -l _ _ _ _ _ (5,5)

VOCABULARY EXTENSION

1. **Read the comments. Supposing they were at the opening of videos about fame, which would you be most likely to watch?**

   1. He was an <u>innovator</u>. A lot of his ideas are just part of everyday life now, but they began with him.
   2. Don't believe anyone who tells you there's a <u>formula</u> to becoming a famous influencer.
   3. Some famous people complain about the <u>invasion of their privacy</u> by the media, but I'm not very sympathetic. If you're lucky enough to have <u>a following</u>, of course journalists will <u>grab any opportunity</u> to gossip about your private life.
   4. Success relies on contacts in the end. If you don't know someone who can <u>fix you up with</u> that interview or audition, you're unlikely to make the big time.
   5. 'Nepobabies' – people whose parents are famous – have an advantage in things like acting and music. It's <u>the same old story</u> – it's not what you know, but who you know.
   6. Their success and fame as a band was due to <u>great teamwork</u>. It's easy to underestimate how important that is.
   7. Her last film was a <u>radical</u> change from her usual roles – <u>out of the blue</u>, she showed she's brilliant at comedy.

2. **Find underlined words or phrases in Exercise 1 that mean the same as 1–5.**

   1. a plan or method that is used to achieve something
   2. very big and important change
   3. something that keeps repeating
   4. a group of people who support, admire, or believe in a particular person, group, or idea
   5. provide someone with something that they need

   Find underlined words or phrases in Exercise 1 that mean the opposite of 6–10.

   6. someone who has no original ideas
   7. respect someone's personal life
   8. ineffective collaboration
   9. something expected
   10. fail to take advantage of a situation

3. **Complete the text with the words in the box.**

   > glamour grab iconic (x2) infamous invade limelight stardom

   Think for a moment of a photograph. It could be of a film star or an ¹_____ historical moment. Now ask yourself if you know the name of the photographer. No? That's no accident. Many photographers prefer to stay out of the ²_____ because being anonymous gives them better access to people and situations. Some of the most ³_____ photos of famous people are those that show them as normal human beings, a long way from the public image associated with ⁴_____ and ⁵_____. On the other hand, the ⁶_____ 'paparazzi' side of photography exists to ⁷_____ people's privacy and ⁸_____ any opportunity for photos of the rich and famous, even in upsetting or tragic situations.

   → **YOUR TURN**

   4. **Find two more new words to describe being famous. Write them here, with a translation or a description of the meaning.**

TOWARDS PROFICIENCY

TOWARDS PROFICIENCY 1

COMPOUND ADJECTIVES

1 **Read the conversation between three friends. Who do you think enjoyed the series the most?**

   A: So what did you think of *Fillings*?
   B: You mean that comedy about Jake, that <u>very impulsive</u> boy who starts a sandwich shop?
   C: Yeah, that's it. He's not very sensible, but you can tell he <u>wants to help</u> people.
   A: I don't agree about him not being sensible, he's <u>thought carefully</u> about his business.
   B: True, but he has a <u>very high opinion of himself</u>, so I don't really like him.
   C: The funniest thing is that his rich uncle won't help him with the business, he's <u>so mean</u>!
   A: Yes! He's definitely the best character.

2 **Read the conversation between three students discussing a film they watched for their course. Who is most critical of the script?**

   A: It's a brilliant example of dialogue.
   B: For me, it was <u>too obvious</u>, like the writer is telling you what to think.
   C: Really? I had a different impression. Like she's trying to <u>show you both sides</u> of the story.
   B: Of course, she's <u>very good at her work</u>, but I still have my doubts.
   A: I thought the final scenes were incredible, I was <u>absolutely amazed</u> by that last conversation.
   C: It certainly comes as a shock to learn that he's <u>a killer with no regrets at all</u>.

3 **Read the conversation about a character in a film. Does A think the character is interesting?**

   A: So, she's a lawyer – she's <u>really observant</u> and doesn't miss anything.
   B: Like lawyers are supposed to!
   A: And she's smart – she realizes who the murderer is because he <u>doesn't anticipate the consequences of</u>…!
   B: Hey! No spoilers!
   A: Sorry, <u>I won't say anything else</u>.
   B: But do you like her, as a character?
   A: Not much. She's not very empathetic, and <u>doesn't care about criticism</u> of how she does things.

4 **Replace the underlined phrases in Exercises 1–3 with a compound adjective in the boxes. Each exercise uses compound adjectives from the same box.**

   big-headed clear-headed hot-headed
   kind-hearted tight-fisted

   cold-blooded even-handed heavy-handed
   open-mouthed sure-footed

   eagle-eyed short-sighted thick-skinned
   tight-lipped

5 **Many compound adjectives use parts of the body to describe character, behaviour or personality. Read the job-suitability questionnaire. How you would answer the questions? Can you guess the job the questions relate to?**

   1 Do your friends ever describe you as kind-hearted?
   2 Have you ever solved a problem between people by being even-handed?
   3 Would you describe yourself as clear-headed when there is a serious problem?
   4 Are you ever told you tend to be hot-headed?
   5 In your opinion, is it acceptable to be big-headed if you manage a group of people?
   6 Would you say you are sufficiently thick-skinned to not get upset by negative criticism?
   7 If something scary is happening, are you good at keeping tight lipped?
   8 If you have learned and memorized a process, are you sure-footed when you implement it?
   9 Have you ever been told you're heavy-handed when you have disagreements with people?
   10 How eagle-eyed are you?

   Score two points if you answered yes to questions 1, 2, 3, 6, 7, 8 and 10 and no to questions 4, 5 and 9. Deduct two points if you answered no to questions 1, 2, 3, 6, 7, 8 and 10 or yes to questions 4, 5, and 9.
   The maximum score is 20 points. For this job you need more than 16 points.

OVER TO YOU

6 **The questionnaire identifies the skills of a good airline cabin crew manager. Choose three of the expressions from this page and write sentences about yourself, or someone you know, who you think would be suitable for this role.**

TOWARDS PROFICIENCY 2

FOOD, EATING AND TASTE IDIOMS

1 Read the article from a film website. Would you be interested in seeing this film?

HOME   **ARTICLES**

First Course/Last Course is a new movie release. We asked our readers what they thought about the film, on the condition that they use food expressions when giving their opinion! This elicited the 'feast' of responses below.

As with any story about secret international organizations, you have to take the plot with <u>a pinch of salt</u>. Having said that, it's gripping, even if for me the ending <u>left a bad taste</u>. No spoilers though. Let's just say it's not exactly a happy ending.

The novel <u>sold like hot cakes</u> – it was top of the best-seller charts for months – and I was sure the film would be disappointing in comparison. However, I have to <u>eat humble pie</u>, as the director might even have improved on the book.

First Course/Last Course is going to be the flop of the year. I'm a great fan of the director Anne Bower's work, so realizing how bad this movie is was <u>a bitter pill to swallow</u>. The novel has a really complex plot, so perhaps Bower just <u>bit off more than she could chew</u>.

For once, our hero, Detective Janine, fails to understand the dangers because she thinks she <u>has bigger fish to fry</u> and leaves her junior assistant to solve the case. I won't <u>spill the beans</u>, but be ready for a surprise!

The film deals with some difficult themes related to loyalty and responsibilities, but never tries to <u>sugarcoat</u> them. It's true to life. Oh, and <u>the icing on the cake</u> – the plot is fantastic!

---

2 Match the underlined phrases in the review to the definitions 1–10.

1. not completely believe something you are told, because it is unlikely to be true
2. something that is very unpleasant but must be accepted
3. admit that you were wrong
4. try to do something that is too difficult
5. something that makes a good situation even better
6. be bought quickly and in large numbers
7. make something seem more positive or pleasant than it really is
8. have an unpleasant memory of something
9. tell people secret information
10. have something more important to do

3 Match an idiom in Exercise 1 to lines from the script of *First Course/Last Course*.

1. 'I never really trusted you Max, but I know now I was wrong. You're my most loyal friend.'
2. 'Denise thought the plan was going to be easy, but how wrong she was!'
3. 'Not only did we get paid really well for our work, but he gave me gold watch as a gift!'
4. 'You're a good worker, Martin, but unfortunately, I have to fire you.'
5. 'I think it's time you told us exactly what's going on – and I mean everything.'
6. 'Bill isn't attending this meeting because he has to report to the director.'
7. 'Martin didn't expect to lose his job, it came as a shock, and he's really upset.'
8. 'I know we had to do it – there wasn't any choice – but I still feel bad about it.'
9. 'She has the best take-away in town, but get there early, before the food sells out!'
10. 'He'll tell you stories about how hard things were in the old days, but he exaggerates so don't think it's all true.'

OVER TO YOU

4 Think of three situations in your life. Write three sentences about them using expressions from this page.

TOWARDS PROFICIENCY 3

COMMUNICATION EXPRESSIONS AND IDIOMS

1 Match the underlined phrases in 1–10 with the similar ideas a–j.

1 'It's so embarrassing – I called you Sheila, but of course she's your sister. I'm always getting muddled up.'
2 'I kept on telling them the weather forecast was for rain and we shouldn't have a picnic, but as usual, what I said fell on deaf ears.'
3 'I'm so tired of his bad manners that this time I put my foot down and insisted he say sorry.'
4 'I've got to get this off my chest – I'm angry because this plan is totally impractical.'
5 'I was absolutely speechless when they told me I'd won.'
6 'Can I butt in here and ask you some more questions?'
7 'We've narrowed down the possible winners to a shortlist we agree on.'
8 'Vicky's got an amazing memory – she told them what they had said word for word.'
9 'I'm sorry – it just slipped out – has that spoiled the surprise?'
10 'What he did speaks volumes about what a good friend he is.'

a He has a habit of interrupting people.
b We began with a long list of options, but finally decided on five.
c She didn't know what to say when the told her their decision.
d Nobody paid any attention to her warnings.
e He felt it was important to tell them why he was upset.
f He didn't mean to reveal the winner, but he mentioned her name.
g She repeated exactly what was said at the meeting.
h The way he helped us when we had problems tells you a lot about his character.
i He frequently confuses people's names.
j She refused to continue until he apologized.

2 You are part of a group responsible for planning an outdoor charity event. Complete the comments made by team members with a phrase in the box.

> butting in   fall on deaf ears
> got that off his chest   muddled up
> narrowed it down   put my foot down
> slipped out   word for word

1 We've _____ the times of the musical performances on the programme – the band comes on after the singer, not the other way round!
2 Max is frustrated by not having enough people to help him – he _____ in the last team meeting.
3 I _____ and insisted that the local council provides extra rubbish collection.
4 The venue was supposed to be a secret, but I'm afraid it just _____ when I was talking to some friends.
5 I've prepared an opening speech I think will motivate people – I've spent a lot of time rehearsing it and know it _____ now.
6 I was explaining the safety procedures to the volunteers, but Ray kept _____ and in the end I had to ask him to wait until I'd finished.
7 We had several people who wanted to be in charge of the social media campaign, but we've _____ to two who we want to work together.
8 I stressed the importance of having a paperless event, and my message didn't _____. Everyone is going to make a big effort in this respect.

3 Work in pairs. Discuss how important you think 1–8 are to having a successful event.

OVER TO YOU

4 Think of situations when you felt communication was effective and clear, or other situations when it was not. Write three sentences describing your experience using expressions from this page.

TOWARDS PROFICIENCY 4

PROGRESS AND PROCESS: METAPHORS, IDIOMS AND EXPRESSIONS

Metaphorical expressions explain a new idea by referring to situations and experiences we are familiar with. We can talk about making or not making progress and finding ways of reaching our objectives with idioms and expressions based on physical movement and journeys.

1 Look at the sentence pairs 1–11. Which uses the underlined expression metaphorically, A or B?

1. A When you come to a crossroads, make sure you turn to the right.
   B When we came to a crossroads it was crucial to make the right choice for the future.
2. A I make a point of taking a walk in the park every evening before going home.
   B We expected the project to take much longer than it did. Actually, it was a walk in the park.
3. A There has definitely been significant improvement, but we are not out of the woods yet.
   B I hope it doesn't start raining because it will be another hour before we are out of the woods.
4. A Asking people to make an extra effort is fine, but making them work at the weekend is going too far.
   B I think we probably passed the store a few minutes ago and we've gone too far.
5. A That was definitely a bumpy ride, but the pilots are specially trained for landing at the airport.
   B Our open day event was a great success, but getting everything ready on time was a bumpy ride.
6. A I'm not sure where things went wrong – perhaps if we retrace our steps we'll find the mistake.
   B I don't think we're lost. If we just retrace our steps we'll find our way back.
7. A I came to the end of the road, but I wasn't sure which direction he said I should take.
   B The partners decided they had come to the end of the road, and it was time to close the business.
8. A We have some important deadlines to meet and I'm afraid that one or two of you are trailing behind.
   B Whenever we go for walks, he trails behind and we have to wait for him.
9. A If you leave right now, you should catch up with Jackie on the way to the train station.
   B I've been sleeping very badly recently because the stress of exams has caught up with me.
10. A My advice would be steer clear of those questions. They'll only complicate things.
    B I advise you to steer clear of the city centre, as there is a lot of traffic.
11. A You'll get there much faster if you take this shortcut and avoid the city centre.
    B For this task we can take a shortcut by using data from an earlier project.

2 Match the definitions below to a metaphorical expression from Exercise 1.

a a quicker way of doing something in order to save time or effort
b avoid a problem or obstacle
c be easy and without problems
d behave in a way that upsets or annoys people
e fail to do something fast enough or on time
f have a difficult time
g make an important decision choosing from a number of options
h not having a problem or difficulty any longer
i repeat a series of things you did previously
j something bad that has been happening begins to cause problems for you
k the point at which it is no longer possible to continue with a process or activity

OVER TO YOU

3 Think of situations when you were trying to make progress or participating in a project of process. Write three sentences describing your experience using expressions from this page.

TOWARDS PROFICIENCY 5

EXPRESSING IDEAS: OPPOSITES AND SYNONYMS

1 🔊 **TP5.1 Listen to two friends talking about a film called *Time Splits*. Put the words and phrases below in the order you hear them.**

appealing ___   plead guilty ___
ally ___   a total mess ___
modesty ___   well-dressed ___
a nobody ___

2 🔊 **TP5.1 Listen again. Match the words and phrases in Exercise 1 to their opposites 1–7.**

1 big fish   5 spotless
2 off-putting   6 plead innocent
3 scruffy   7 rival
4 vanity

DISAGREEING BY USING OPPOSITES

3 Use one of the words or phrases in Exercise 2 to write a response that disagrees with what the first speaker says. The first is done for you as an example.

1 Max told me that his uncle is a big fish in the music business.
I heard that as well, but in fact, he's a nobody.
2 Look at the photo of this amazing dessert – isn't that appealing?
3 Is your cousin the well-dressed guy over there?
4 Did you say something about his vanity?
5 Just look at your room. What happened? It's spotless!
6 There's a rumour that the robber who was arrested is going to plead guilty.
7 I read something about how they were great rivals when they were young.

4 We often use synonyms to express agreement with people.

A: The film wasn't what I'd expected at all – it seemed kind of slow.
B: Yes, I felt it dragged as well.
(slow = dragged)
A: Let's make an effort to get together with the others this weekend, it's ages since we did.
B: I totally agree – let's try to meet up.
(get together = meet up)

Complete the dialogues 1–5 with the words and phrases in the box. You do not need all the words and phrases.

> a change of scene   on the bright side
> committed   unexpected   put my foot down
> slipped out   guarantee

1 A: How about going for a walk somewhere different? We've been here for hours.
B: Yes, _____ could be good.
2 A: What a surprising ending!
B: Yeah! Completely _____.
3 A: I don't think he's really _____ to this new job.
B: No, I sense he doesn't believe in what he's doing.
4 A: There's no _____ the experiment is going to work.
B: True. We can't take it for granted.
5 A: What I like about her most is her optimism.
B: It's true. She always looks _____.

OVER TO YOU

5 Imagine two situations where you might want to be diplomatic. Write sentences using an opposite adjective.

Think of two comments friends have made recently you agreed with. Write a reply to their comments using a synonym.

TOWARDS PROFICIENCY 6
FRIENDSHIPS AND RELATIONSHIPS

1 Read the extracts from a novel about how friendships are formed and change over time. Which character do you find most interesting – Brenda, Will or Ana? Why?

Extract 1

From the day they met at high school, Brenda and Will had been <u>inseparable</u>. They were not an obvious combination. Brenda was very sociable and chatty, made friends easily and could always find ways of making the best of any situation. Will was shy and didn't like the limelight, but they formed <u>a bond</u> they felt could not be broken. However, that summer, something completely unexpected <u>came between</u> them. And it all started with a silly argument about pizza.

Extract 2

'This is crazy,' exclaimed Ana. 'You guys are – well – as close as anyone I know. I've always wanted to have someone like Brenda in my life – someone who always <u>has your back</u>. So, you two <u>not being on speaking terms</u> just doesn't make sense.'
'I know,' said Will, 'you're right, but I don't know how to <u>patch things up</u>.'
'And you've come me for advice. Right? If you have a problem, ask Ana?'
'I guess so,' said Will, with a guilty smile.

Extract 3

Ana found it hard to make friends. She knew she was liked and respected – the 'clever' one of the group, but she didn't really <u>click</u> with people in ways that formed a strong bond. Most of her friendships were a bit <u>rocky</u>. She was also a bit unwilling to trust people after her old friend Larisa, who she thought would always <u>stick by her</u>, turned out to be <u>a fair-weather friend</u>. They had a lot of fun together but when things got difficult for Ana, Larisa just disappeared.

2 Match the underlined words and phrases in Exercise 1 to the definitions 1–9. One defintion corresponds to two phrases.

1. having no communication at all
2. someone who is only friend when things are going well
3. support and defend (x2)
4. repair a relationship
5. always together
6. difficult and unpredictable
7. a strong connection
8. harm the relationship between two or more people
9. when two people like each other immediately

3 Complete the quiz with a word or phrase in the box.

> bond   clicked   fair-weather friend
> have your back   inseparable
> on speaking terms   patch things up   rocky

What kind of FRIEND are you?

1. Are you more likely to form a _____ with someone if you share an interest in sport or music?
2. Is there someone you spend so much time with that people describe you as _____?
3. When you've had a major disagreement with a friend, how easy is it for you to _____ with them?
4. Have you ever met someone for the first time and you just _____, as if you had known each other for years?
5. Has anyone accused you of being a _____ because they felt you didn't help them when they needed it?
6. Have you ever had a _____ relationship with a friend, but remained close despite your problems?
7. How many of your friends are you sure would _____ if you needed help and support?
8. Is there anyone you used to consider a good friend who you are currently not _____ with? Do you hope you can be friends again in the future?

OVER TO YOU

4 Write a short answer to three of the quiz questions in Exercise 3. Use three expressions from this page in your answer.

IRREGULAR VERBS

Infinitive	Past simple	Past participle	Translation	Infinitive	Past simple	Past participle	Translation
be	was/were	been		leave	left	left	
beat	beat	beaten		lend	lent	lent	
become	became	become		let	let	let	
begin	began	begun		lie	lied	lied	
bite	bit	bitten		light	lit	lit	
bleed	bled	bled		lose	lost	lost	
blow	blew	blown		make	made	made	
break	broke	broken		mean	meant	meant	
bring	brought	brought		meet	met	met	
build	built	built		pay	paid	paid	
burn	burned/burnt	burned/burnt		put	put	put	
buy	bought	bought		read	read	read	
catch	caught	caught		ride	rode	ridden	
choose	chose	chosen		ring	rang	rung	
come	came	come		rise	rose	risen	
cost	cost	cost		run	ran	run	
cut	cut	cut		say	said	said	
dig	dug	dug		see	saw	seen	
do	did	done		sell	sold	sold	
draw	drew	drawn		send	sent	sent	
dream	dreamed/dreamt	dreamed/dreamt		shine	shone	shone	
drink	drank	drunk		shoot	shot	shot	
drive	drove	driven		show	showed	shown	
eat	ate	eaten		shut	shut	shut	
fall	fell	fallen		sing	sang	sung	
feel	felt	felt		sit	sat	sat	
fight	fought	fought		sleep	slept	slept	
find	found	found		speak	spoke	spoken	
fly	flew	flown		spell	spelled/spelt	spelled/spelt	
forget	forgot	forgotten		spend	spent	spent	
get	got	got		stand	stood	stood	
give	gave	given		steal	stole	stolen	
go	went	gone		swim	swam	swum	
grow	grew	grown		take	took	taken	
hang	hung	hung		teach	taught	taught	
have	had	had		tear	tore	torn	
hear	heard	heard		tell	told	told	
hide	hid	hidden		think	thought	thought	
hit	hit	hit		throw	threw	thrown	
hold	held	held		understand	understood	understood	
hurt	hurt	hurt		wake	woke	woken	
keep	kept	kept		wear	wore	worn	
know	knew	known		win	won	won	
lead	led	led		write	wrote	written	
learn	learned/learnt	learned/learnt					

Acknowledgements

The authors and publishers acknowledge the following sources of copyright material and are grateful for the permissions granted. While every effort has been made, it has not always been possible to identify the sources of all the material used, or to trace all copyright holders. If any omissions are brought to our notice, we will be happy to include the appropriate acknowledgements on reprinting and in the next update to the digital edition, as applicable.

The publishers are grateful to the following contributors: EMC Design Ltd, text design and layouts; Daniel Summersgill, cover design; Sonica Studios, audio recordings; Ruth Cox and Melanie Starren, Editorial work; Tom Bradbury, Jill Buggey and Bartosz Michałowski exam reviewers.

Keys: U = Unit, ES = Employability Skills, VB = Vocabulary Builder, TP = Towards Proficiency.

Photography

All the photographs are sourced from Getty Images.

U1: ferrantraite/E+; oleg66/E+; Antonio Busiello/Moment; Europa Press News; Jordi Janau/Moment; Maskot; Marco Di Lauro/Getty Images News; Kris Timken/Tetra images; Olga Smolina/Moment; **U2:** SolStock/E+; kali9/E+; Ricardo Mendoza Garbayo/Moment; JohnnyGreig/E+; **U3:** Pornpimon Rodchua/iStock; LynaStock/DigitalVision Vectors; Alena Matrosova/500Px Plus; GoodLifeStudio/E+; Westend61; **U4:** alvaro gonzalez/Moment; Carey Kirkella/DigitalVision; TwilightShow/E+; Morsa Images/DigitalVision; Zoran Zeremski/iStock/Getty Images Plus; Anchiy/E+; **U5:** kadirkaba/DigitalVision Vectors; MirageC/Moment; Joe McBride/The Image Bank; Kseniya Starkova/Moment; Oscar Wong/Moment; **U6:** Westend61; Olga Pankova/Moment; FatCamera/E+; **U7:** Peter Harrison/Stone; golero/E+; Tim Graham/Stone; Jose Colon/Getty Images News; **U8:** CasarsaGuru/E+; **U9:** Chawkaew Poungpeth/E+; Robert Daly/OJO Images; **ES:** Sean Gladwell/Moment; Floresco Productions/OJO Images; rolandtopor/iStock/Getty Images Plus; Ginnet Delgado/iStock/Getty Images Plus; SrdjanPav/E+; LeoPatrizi/E+; FG Trade/E+; Tang Ming Tung/DigitalVision; monkeybusinessimages/iStock/Getty Images Plus; **VB:** Victor Habbick Visions/Science Photo Library; **TP:** PS Photography/Moment; Wavebreakmedia/iStock/Getty Images Plus; Westend61; PM Images/DigitalVision; Maskot.

Cover photography by AaronAmat/iStock/Getty Images.

Video

Video production by Silversun Media Group.

Audio

Audios produced by Sonica Studios Ltd.

Typeset

Typesetting by EMC Design Ltd.

URLs

The publisher has used its best endeavours to ensure that the URLs for external websites referred to in this book are correct and active at the time of going to press. However, the publisher has no responsibility for the websites and can make no guarantee that a site will remain live or that the content is or will remain appropriate.